How They Make It Work...
21 Habits of a
Successful Marriage

Ed Wimberly, PhD

A Practical Guide to Healthier Relationships

ISBN 978-1-0980-0405-7 (paperback)
ISBN 978-1-0980-0435-4 (digital)

Christian Faith Publishing, Inc.
832 Park Avenue
Meadville, PA 16335
www.christianfaithpublishing.com

Printed in the United States of America

Contents

Introduction

Throughout the course of my forty-five years in private practice, I have worked with many struggling individuals who were willing to do the hard work it takes to minimize the effects of painful past experiences and to chart a new path for their lives.

I have also had the good fortune of spending more than many hours with couples who were struggling to make positive changes in their relationships. As a result of my observing, as well as being privileged to be an intimate part of their struggles, it has become clear to me that usually when a couple sets out to make improvements to their relationship, their first and primary focus is on what's broken and what needs to be eliminated in order to improve. Typically, their initial focus is on what's wrong (usually, what's wrong with the other person!), and what's working against the success and satisfaction they both desire. They then strive to eliminate the problem, understandably thinking their relationship will then be "fixed."

If it's a critical nature, they work toward being less critical; if a short fuse and anger is eating away at the passion and excitement that was once fundamental to their relationship, they address it and do everything they can to eliminate it; if selfishness is the culprit, they work on getting rid of it.

If impatience has taken a toll on their once healthy relationship, they make an effort to be less impatient; if irresponsible spending patterns have crept in, they strive to be more responsible and accountable in their expenditures.

The number of destructive patterns that can undermine a once healthy marriage is very close to endless, and there is certainly nothing wrong with working on what needs to be eliminated in an effort to improve our relationship. In fact, it is necessary to do so and could be argued that it is a good place to start.

But it is only the start.

Typically, the complaints that couples come in with and label, "the problems," are not the real problems at all, but rather, the symptoms of underlying issues they are either unaware of or deny their importance. Certainly, their initial complaints are problematic and must be addressed, but I suggest to them that they are "symptomatic problems" that will likely return if the underlying issues are not addressed. A fair analogy might be cutting off a weed at the surface; it may look good for a time, but if the root system is not eliminated, the weed will grow back.

I make it a practice to follow up my work with couples by occasionally reconnecting in order to see how they are doing in their continued efforts to improve the quality of their relationship. There are many who report a continued improvement beyond what they achieved in therapy, then there are those who have either fallen back into their old and dysfunctional habits or at best, stalled in their progress.

As a result of my follow-up conversations, I have become acutely aware of a significant difference that sets the continued success of some apart from the couples who seem to slide back into their self-defeating habits.

It has become clear that those who continued to improve were those who had not only eliminated the unhealthy habits that motivated them to seek help but also replaced those habits with new and improved ones.

Those who had fallen back into old self-defeating habits were usually the ones who, although they had initially succeeded in getting rid of unhealthy habits, stopped short of replacing them with new and improved ones.

It is not unlike digging a hole to plant a tree. If we dig that hole but stop short of replacing the dirt with a plant, then over time, the wind and rain wash the removed dirt right back in.

So the purpose of what follows is to consider and possibly implement what it takes to keep the passion and excitement alive in our relationship in the midst of the complexities that inevitably come with the passage of time. In broad terms, our goal is two-fold:

First, to identify any habits in our relationship that might be working against us and to then replace them with new and healthy ones;

Second, to gain insight into some of the life experiences we have had that may be a source of the self-defeating habits that need to be eliminated. While cutting the weed off at the surface is necessary and in the short term helpful, digging out the root system further helps assure that it will not return. Only then are we able to enjoy a degree of the original passion that motivated and drew us together in the early days of our relationship.

What follows is just a bit of what I have learned from some wonderful and hardworking people who caught the vision to not only eliminate the unhealthy habits but to follow up with replacing those habits with new and mutually satisfying healthy ones.

Most books are written to be read from cover to cover. And if it is a particularly good book and you are a voracious reader, you may even finish it in one rainy-day sitting. I suggest with this one that you take your time, read the habits in no particular order, and focus on the ones that stand out as especially relevant to your relationship.

And as you read, keep in mind that very few healthy marriages do well all the time with all of the twenty-one habits that will be suggested here. What makes them healthy is not that they have gained perfection in each and every one but that they not only know where their strengths are but where they need to focus in order to improve where they are struggling.

So be encouraged, knowing it is the process and effort toward improving that makes the difference rather than the achievement of perfection; it is a journey, not a destination.

Following each of the twenty-one habits of a healthy marriage suggested here, you will find several questions that are designed to help in your journey of replacing any unhealthy habits with more beneficial ones. If your relationship is on a stable footing and just in need of occasional fine tuning, you might consider discussing them together and on your own. If you are struggling just to survive, consider addressing them with a trained third party rather than without assistance.

Allow me to make one additional suggestion for you to consider as you read: it is tempting for any of us to believe that the changes needed in order to improve our relationship are the ones required of the other person rather than of us. "If he/she would just get their act together, then our relationship would improve." While it may be that changes in the other person would help, I encourage you to focus more on yourself instead of your spouse and how he/she needs to consider new habits. When both of you are willing to look honestly at the part you play rather than seeing yourself as the victim of the others' faults, then the stage is set for real and significant progress.

I hope what you are about to consider makes a difference in your relationship.

Ed Wimberly, Ph.D.
Docedwimberly@gmail.com

*Couples in healthy marriages pick their battles —
and they do it well.*

Habit #1

Couples in a Healthy Marriage Ask the Question "Does It Really Matter?" Before Reacting

The twenty-one habits of a healthy marriage I will suggest to you are not in any particular order of importance. That said, I do believe that none of the twenty-one that will help insure a healthy marriage relationship is more important than this first one.

Many a battle is waged over things that in the long run really don't matter—at least not much. In fact, very often in warfare, the underlying motivation is simply to win. And ironically through the course of warfare, it is common that neither side actually gains much

11

of anything. In fact, it could be argued that usually more is lost than gained on both sides of a conflict.

Perhaps there would be more peace in our world all around if the question, "Does it really matter?" were asked more frequently before doing battle. A conclusion I have personally come to through the course of far more years than I would like to admit, is that fewer things really matter, but the things that do matter, matter more to me. I could have no doubt avoided many conflicts over the years if I had learned this earlier in life.

In healthy and growing marriages, both make it a habit to first consider just how important their gripe, criticism, or complaint really is before bringing it up as an issue. And usually, they get it right; while they are able to disregard and set aside what really is of little importance, they are more able and willing to express and address those issues that could do harm if not dealt with and worked through.

Interestingly, many couples who are struggling and have an unhealthy marriage do actually ask the question, "Does it really matter?" But invariably, they come up with the wrong answer! Too often the issues that really should matter—those that need attention and discussion—are ignored, set aside, and placed into the "Screw it! It doesn't really matter!" category. And it is usually with a destructive attitude of hurt, anger, and resentment that the significant but ignored issue is declared unimportant and then set aside (sweeping "it" under the carpet comes to mind). In turn, those issues that are really unimportant that could be disregarded become the focal point and reason for a battle.

Unfortunately, there is no master list that I know of that we can turn to in deciding whether or not an issue or complaint we have is important enough to address. I suppose if there were such a list, life might be easier.

I recall several years ago in a workshop I was leading, suggesting the importance of asking this question before deciding whether or not to address it with one's spouse. I remember rhetorically asking,

"Does it *really* matter that she doesn't always turn the light off when she leaves a room?" I suggested that perhaps the better response could be to (with a good attitude) simply get up and turn off the light for her.

I followed up with another rhetorical question: "Does it *really* matter that he leaves the seat of the toilet up after using it?"

A young woman in the back of the room quickly and with great enthusiasm raised her hand and declared, "Oh, it matters! It *really* matters!"

I explained that there really isn't an absolute and indisputable list of what legitimately should matter and what should not. What matters to one person may not matter to another. And for this young lady, there probably was a very good reason why putting the toilet seat down when finished mattered (I restrained myself and didn't ask for details).

The key is to seriously and honestly consider the legitimacy of our complaint before making it an issue worthy of dispute. And it can be helpful to take an honest look back and ask why our issue or complaint matters so much when maybe it should not. Doing so could prove beneficial since the prior experiences, observations, relationships, and messages we heard and absorbed early on can influence and help shape what we believe matters in our life today.

Why do couples in unhealthy relationships seem so often to go to battle over things that often don't matter in the long run?

Pride, the need to win, the desire to control, the misconception that doing things my way translates into my being loved, needing my spouse to be just like me—these are but a few of the more common underlying motivations for making an issue of small complaints or frustrations that, truth be told, really should not matter or lead to conflict.

Healthy marriages make it a habit to pick their battles, and they do it well. And by doing so, they appropriately ignore what is not important while dealing with the issues that really do matter and need attending to.

Try asking "Does it really matter?" before responding for a while and see what happens.

Questions to Consider

1. What is an issue in your relationship that matters to you, that when brought up, usually leads to an argument or conflict?

2. Do you know why this issue matters to you as much as it does?

3. Are there any issues that you believe matter to you that, if you were honest, shouldn't really matter?

4. Is there anything you believe really matters, but rather than addressing it, you keep to yourself?

5. If so, what might be the motivation behind your ignoring what should be addressed (fear, lazy, believing it wouldn't help to address it)?

6. On a scale of 1–10 (10, excellent), how are you doing?

   1___2___3___4___5___6___7___8___9___10___

7. How do you think your spouse is doing?

   1___2___3___4___5___6___7___8___9___10___

They avoid holding grudges.

Habit #2

They Avoid Grudges by Keeping Short Accounts

During a tribute to his life-long friend, George H.W. Bush, Senator Allen Simpson recalled a quote his mother often repeated: "Anger corrodes the container it is carried in." The same could be said of grudges that are held; grudges do indeed corrode the container they are carried in. When they are carried over time in a marriage, that relationship becomes corroded.

There's nothing like a grudge to drive a wedge between two people in an otherwise healthy and satisfying relationship. Whether it is between two professionals in business together, a friendship, or one between a parent and their child, grudges held over time can damage and even destroy relationships.

And there is probably no relationship that can be more damaged by the accumulation of grudges than the marriage relationship.

And the irony is that the resulting fallout can do more lasting damage than any done in other less important relationships.

When we hold a grudge in other relationships, we can more easily avoid that person, end the relationship, or shrug off the issue as not really being that important. But in our marriage, he/she is there when we go to bed, and they are there when we wake up; they are there across the table at dinner, and they are there when we retire to the TV room. They are there on Friday night at the beginning of our weekend, and they are there Sunday night as our weekend winds down. So ignoring or minimizing an unspoken grudge in our continually present marriage relationship is a far more difficult one than in any of our other relationships.

And in addition to their consistent presence, a small grudge that we ignore can be further aggravated by other frustrating events that might occur. And before you know it, well, what might have started out as just a little mole hill turns into a mountain.

Husbands and wives who want to protect their marriage from the potential destruction of unspoken resentment and frustrations work to develop the habit of keeping short accounts with each other; they address whatever it is that is bothering them in order to clear the air. Of course, it is important to first consider whether the issue really does matter before addressing it (take a look back on habit #1), but once they determine that it really does matter, they address their concern.

Since dealing with important and potentially grudge-producing issues can have such positive results in our marriage, why is it so difficult to do so for many of us? What interferes with our successfully keeping short accounts? I suppose laziness and simple lack of motivation are both a possibility.

What is more often the case, however, is that there are deeper issues behind the pattern of sweeping under the rug what should actually be brought into the light and addressed. Here are just a few that come to mind:

- Fear of the response I might get.

Some people are simply conflict avoidant, usually because they fear losing the battle so "why borrow trouble?" Or they may fear that doing so might make things worse.

- Fear that airing my grievance will do no good.

"What's the use?" If efforts to address issues have consistently fallen on deaf ears and failed to lead to any significant resolve in the past, then understandably, the lack of success and a string of failures might understandably interfere with the motivation to try—only to once again fail.

- "I have been taught not to complain but to 'suck it up' and to move on."

When a person has a history—especially a childhood history—of being criticized, put down, or punished for complaining or airing a frustration, it is easy for that learned pattern to carry over into their adult relationships. No one wants to be shamed or not taken seriously for having a complaint they feel is legitimate, so if they believe that history might repeat itself, why not just suck it up and move on?

- If I complain, my marriage must have serious flaws.

Put another way, "If it isn't perfect, then our marriage must have serious problems." The misguided belief here is that if we ignore the conflict, maybe it will go away. This reasoning goes hand in hand with the notion that, by putting off a yearly physical check-up, we can avoid the possibility of bad news. To do so, we certainly are able to avoid any immediate fear or pain (ignorance is bliss, comes to mind). But then, the consequence of our denial is that we miss the possibility of eliminating any immediate problem and other secondary ills and difficulties might later develop as a result.

- If I complain, then I must be selfish.

This too can be a carry-over from early childhood experiences and messages. When a child grows up in a home where the standard responses to their childhood complaints were "Stop being so selfish," then chances are more likely that as an adult, they may favor avoiding and stuffing their grievances over addressing them. Understandably but unfortunately, resisting the label of "selfish" may take precedence over the importance of avoiding grudges by keeping short accounts.

There are, no doubt, other understandable but unfortunate life experiences that can make keeping short accounts difficult. Whatever the reasons for doing so, it is important to consider the damage over time that may occur in doing so.

Simply stated, there is no room in a healthy marriage for holding a grudge, and the only way to avoid doing so is to keep short accounts about the things that really matter.

Questions to Consider

1. Are you aware of any grudges you might be holding against your spouse?

2. Do you ever wonder if your spouse is holding a grudge against you?

3. If there are grudges in your relationship, how are they affecting your relationship?

4. If you are holding a grudge, are you willing to address it?

5. If not, do you know why not (fear, don't want to complain, futile)?

6. On a scale of 1–10 (10, excellent), how are you doing?

    1___2___3___4___5___6___7___8___9___10___

7. How do you think your spouse is doing?

    1___2___3___4___5___6___7___8___9___10___

They are willing to go beyond just "sorry."

Habit #3

They Are Willing to Say, "I'm Sorry, Will You Forgive Me?"

Have you ever noticed that more often than not when a child is corrected by their parent and then asked to say they are sorry, how difficult it is for them to comply? And when they do, it is usually a weak and reluctant "Sorry"—likely a word repeated because it is required more than a reflection of true sincerity.

And usually if it is required at all by the authority figure, it's like pulling teeth to get them to use the personal pronoun *I*. I suspect that one reason might be because avoiding "I" protects their ego just a bit and helps distance them in their own minds from any possible responsibility for what they have just been corrected for.

If a parent does succeed in getting the accused to actually own their behavior with the addition of the personal pronoun, this is usually where the process ends. Seldom does a parent insist that their kids actually ask if the person wronged will forgive them. At first glance, this might sound like an unnecessary step in the reconciliation process but is actually a very important step taken in healthy marriages.

The point and importance of following an apology (not just "sorry," but "I am sorry") with the closing question "Will you forgive me?" is that in doing so, the truly repentant party learns where they stand with the person they have hurt (angered, wronged, etc.). Only then can true reconciliation occur.

So this last step in the forgiveness process helps in the goal of reconciliation. And it is this completion that helps bring closure and in turn, minimizes the likelihood of a grudge being held going forward by the person being asked for their forgiveness.

It could be argued that most of us come by the reluctance to apologize honestly. Call it human nature, sin nature, stubborn inclination, or maybe we just were not encouraged to do so by our parents. Whatever the case, saying we are sorry and actually asking that we be forgiven is difficult for most of us.

The simple explanation for our resistance to accepting responsibility for our misdeeds might simply be human nature. Or as an old comedian, Flip Wilson, used to say, "It's not my fault, the devil made me do it." It can seem a safer route to simply avoid responsibility by blaming the devil or others for our misdeeds. But there are two additional road blocks that are common and make repenting and then actually asking for forgiveness so difficult. One is pride and the other is fear of being vulnerable.

Pride

A common reason for our reluctance to apologize is the issue of pride. When we say we are sorry, we are acknowledging weakness or imperfection. While just about all of us know we fall short of perfection, it is somehow another thing to acknowledge that we do to others—especially to the others we care most about.

In most areas of personality development, I place more importance on the influence nurturing plays in our development than I do on the influence of nature. Certainly, nature does play a significant role in who we are, as well as in who we are to become, but I have been far more impressed with the role that nurturing plays in our development over that of nature.

However, in spite of how much more important I believe the nurturing is that we receive than what we are born with genetically, I do believe that pride is one characteristic we are born with and that it is innately present in every human being that has come down the pike.

My belief is based on having observed infants and seen how the presence of pride seems always to show up early on. It seems that this is a characteristic that is present far earlier than others that seem to develop over time. If this is true, it is no wonder that pride can play a significant role in interfering with our ability to say we are sorry and then to actually ask for forgiveness.

Fear of Being Vulnerable

It's one thing to make ourselves a bit vulnerable by saying "Sorry" in a way that is reminiscent of our early childhood efforts. It's a step or two beyond this mild vulnerability when we add the personal pronoun *I*—"I am sorry"—in our effort to wipe the slate clean and start afresh. We become even more vulnerable when we add to "I'm sorry" the all-important question: "Will you forgive me?"

Not just "Sorry;" not just, "I am sorry," but *"I'm sorry. Will you forgive me?"*

That all-important question goes well beyond acknowledging we were wrong when we simply say "Sorry," and to do so requires more vulnerability, so our risk is greater. And yet it is crucial that we do so since asking the question opens the door to bringing closure and reconciliation, something that simply saying "Sorry" does not.

Our resistance to being vulnerable when we take the next step of asking forgiveness may be due to fear of what our spouse might do with their new-found power.

- What if they say, "No, I won't forgive you"?

- What if they demand that I earn their forgiveness?
- Will I be able to do what they want in order to be forgiven?
- Will they try to get even?
- Will they bring it up in the future and in some way use my "crime" against me?
- Will they use my wrong to manipulate me for their own gain?

It is unfortunate and counterproductive to a healthy marriage when some choose to either ignore their mistakes or become defensive in an effort to protect themselves. As a result, they run the risk of damaging the very relationship that started out to be the most important one in their lives. And although it is a normal inclination for most of us humans to avoid the vulnerability required to ask forgiveness when we've blown it, people in healthy marriages make it a habit of overcoming that fear and doing it anyway.

Questions to Consider

1. How easy/difficult is it for you to say you're sorry?

2. When you ask forgiveness, is his/her response usually helpful?

3. Is the idea of actually asking, "Will you forgive me?" difficult?

4. If it is difficult, is it fear, pride, or something else that makes it hard to do?

5. If apologizing and asking forgiveness is difficult for either of you, how is this affecting your relationship?

6. On a scale of 1–10 (10, excellent), how are you doing?

   1___2___3___4___5___6___7___8___9___10___

7. How do you think your spouse is doing?

   1___2___3___4___5___6___7___8___9___10___

They are willing to take the risk of forgiving.

Habit #4

They Understand the Importance of Forgiving

In the previous chapter, a habit found in healthy marriages of saying they are sorry, and then taking the second step of actually asking for forgiveness was addressed. As important and difficult it is to ask forgiveness when we have messed up, it can be every bit as important and difficult to grant forgiveness when we have been hurt. It stands to reason too that the deeper the hurt and the greater the damage, the more difficult it is for us to forgive.

Why Granting Forgiveness Can Be Difficult

And just as there are risks involved with admitting our mistakes, misbehaviors, and misdeeds, so too are there risks and barriers that can make granting forgiveness difficult when we have been hurt or wronged. But if being able and willing to forgive in our marriage can be so constructive and lead to growth and improvement, what makes it so difficult for many of us to do so?

Several understandable but unproductive reasons come to mind:

1. The need to protect ourselves from being hurt again.

There is often the feeling that if we forgive our spouse, then our grace and mercy will make it just that much more likely that the egregious act will happen again; if we forgive too easily, then we may appear weak and unduly tolerant, and thus, a sitting duck for further and repeated "abuse."

There is actually some truth to this notion that as long as we don't forgive, we minimize the possibility of additional hurt. It is a fact that there is protection in not forgiving, but at what cost to the health and well-being of our relationship?

2. The need for revenge.

"Now it's your turn to hurt the way you hurt me" may be the cry of the person wronged. Forgiveness may be an eventual possibility but not until there has been some degree of payment for the unacceptable behaviors. "Since you hurt me, it's now your turn to hurt. There's a price to pay for your crime." Unfortunately, in the gap between revenge and forgiveness, more harm and damage may occur.

3. The belief that regaining trust must precede our ability to forgive.

"If I can't yet trust, then how can I forgive?" The opposite is actually more accurate; in order to trust again, we must first forgive; forgiveness is a *decision*, and it must occur before the *process* of regaining trust can begin.

4. The belief that "If I can't forget, then how can I forgive?"

"Forgive and forget," as the old saying goes, suggests that we should be able to actually forget the misdeeds and mistakes of the other. Well, our forgetting the transgression of another probably won't happen—at least not until sometime well into our nineties when we begin to forget just about everything! Contrary to the popular notion, "How can I forgive if I can't forget?" forgetting is not a prerequisite to forgiving, so it is possible and necessary to do so even though the memory of the unfortunate event lingers. Granted, it is necessary to get beyond our dwelling on the unfortunate event, but actually forgetting it is not only unnecessary in order to forgive, it is not likely to happen.

5.   The baggage of "conflict connection."

If historically our primary means of connecting were through conflict, then the need to perpetuate conflict in our marriage will likely take priority over peace and civility. Under these circumstances, it is understandable but unacceptable that we might resist reconciliation through forgiveness. If forgiveness is granted, then the conflict is resolved; if the conflict is eliminated, then there goes the means of connecting.

The habit of connecting by way of conflict can develop as a result of constant fighting, bickering, and conflicting in one's family of origin. Since we humans have a God-given need to connect with others in one way or another, and we have not been taught to connect by way of healthy interactions but instead have a history of family battle and conflict, then the current life pattern of conflict connection may kick in. After all, "Negative strokes are better than no strokes at all," and this becomes the unconscious battle cry when there is a history of consistently connecting by way of conflict.

Only a very few struggle severely with conflict connection. If you do not, it might be difficult for you to fully understand just how disruptive this baggage can be for some. If you do relate to this, the good news is that the pattern can be broken; if it is not, the effort to connect will continue to take the form of what one has historically become accustomed to with fights, disputes, and conflicts remaining the norm. As long as the conflict persists, there is a distorted sense of connection that is lost if the conflict is resolved. And since one purpose and result of forgiveness is to eliminate the conflict, forgiving the transgressor may be resisted.

6. The belief that if we forgive, we must give up being the victim.

Why, you might ask, would anyone want to hang on to being a victim? While most of us don't exactly relish such a reputation, there are those who do. And the reason for this may go back, as so often it does, to early childhood experiences and messages.

When a child grows up receiving care, protection, love, and nurturing only when they are somehow hurt or in need of being "rescued," then they may come to believe that in their current relationship, the only time they are worthy of being loved, cared for, and nurtured is when they are a victim or in some way in need of being rescued; they have paired being a victim, pitied by others, and in need of being rescued with being loved and cared for.

As a result of this pairing, they are unable to receive what they need emotionally unless it comes in the form of being rescued. And in order to justify being rescued (cared for, loved, attended to), they must remain a victim, and true forgiveness would require that they abandon that position (and as a result, give up their chance to be loved via being rescued). It is complicated and difficult to understand for those who do not struggle with this misconception. Nonetheless it does exist with some.

Forgiveness can be a daunting task. But in spite of how difficult, it is even more challenging to maintain the vibrancy and satisfaction in our relationship when for any reason we carry around the weight of refusing to forgive.

Try it! I think you will like the results.

Questions to Consider

1. How easily are you able to offer forgiveness when it is asked for?

2. If forgiveness does not come easily, do you understand why?

3. Is your spouse able to forgive?

4. For either of you, are there strings attached to your forgiving?

5. If there are strings attached, what is the effect on your relationship?

6. On a scale of 1–10 (10, excellent), how are you doing?

   1___2___3___4___5___6___7___8___9___10___

7. How do you think your spouse is doing?

   1___2___3___4___5___6___7___8___9___10___

They celebrate their differences.

Habit #5

They Appreciate Their
Personality Differences

Wouldn't the world be a better place if everyone were just like me?

Well, no, not really.

Okay, how about this then?

"Wouldn't my marriage be a bit better if we were both, at the very least, just a little more like me?"

Well, no, not really.

And yet, when we resist not only accepting but actually celebrating the differences, isn't that kind of what we are thinking? "If my spouse were just a little more like me, then our relationship might be better." I am reminded of the humorous valentine card that reads, "I love you just the way I am."

I suppose there is more than just a bit to apply here from the Greek mythology where Narcissus saw his face in a pool of water and immediately fell in love with his own reflected image. His reflection was just like him, and he really liked what he saw!

Have you ever noticed that we humans are usually drawn to other people who are most similar to how we see ourselves? Like Narcissus, we tend to be more comfortable with others whose personality characteristics are similar to our own. When another thinks, acts, and feels in similar ways that we do, there tends to be less tension because there is more we agree on. Usually, the more similar we see ourselves, the easier those friendships are to maintain since they tend to be more predictable and fraught with less conflict. Usually we are not drawn as strongly to others who are different than we are.

Differences don't destroy marriages; failure to understand, accept and celebrate them does.

Although significant characteristic and personality differences in a marriage usually make for a more challenging relationship, the real deal breaker is not usually the differences that exist between them. Often in an effort to understand and make sense of a failed marriage, armchair psychologists point to the differences in their personality make-up as the probable cause of the marriage failure, but that isn't always the case.

While personality differences might seem at first glance to be a plausible explanation, the fundamental problem usually has more to do with the fact that neither is willing to put the well-being of their relationship ahead of their personality and characteristic differences. Much like Narcissus's love for himself, our self-image and ego can get in the way of a healthy marriage when we discount and resist embracing and celebrating the differences between ourselves and our spouse.

No man is an island.

Another common roadblock to celebrating and accepting the differences between us may be the unattainable desire some have for a conflict-free relationship, where life can be lived on their terms and with little interference. And so they may set about the task of making their spouse into something that more resembles themselves since, the more similar, the easier it might be to have a conflict-free relationship.

Granted, there is nothing particularly wrong with the desire to live life on your own terms and with no conflict—nothing, that is, if you are the only soul out in the middle of the Pacific somewhere, shipwrecked and living on a deserted island. Then doing what you want, when you want, the way you want, and with no responsibility or accountability to anyone else (since there isn't anyone else!) is doable and reasonable. And at first glance, it may even seem a bit appealing at times. But the day another survivor washes up onto your otherwise deserted and exclusive island, the responsibility of recognizing and respecting the characteristic and personality differences of that newcomer becomes a necessity if you are both to survive.

Don't look now, but another soul washed up onto your deserted island the day you got married.

It does stand to reason that couples who are more similar than they are dissimilar will likely have fewer conflicts to navigate and fewer differences to work through, although certainly other issues may exist. And likewise, it is usually true that the greater the differences we must accept and learn to live with, the more hard work that may be required to have a healthy and satisfying marriage. But those differences do not have to be deal breakers—relationship busters—but can through hard work lead to a satisfying relationship.

So healthy marriages make a habit of celebrating their differences rather than criticizing them or being threatened by them. And they are able to do so because their differences are seen as a way of "growing" an exciting and more fulfilling relationship rather than as a threat to their individual and desired ways of doing things. Although those differences can create tension and difficult times of working through conflict, in the long run, both recognize the value that can be found in being married to someone who is their own person and not just like the person they see when they look in the mirror.

Questions to Consider

1. In general, are you and your spouse more similar or dissimilar?

2. What is one significant difference between your personalities?

3. Do any of the differences ever create tension or conflict between you?

4. If so, what conflicts occur as a result of your personality differences?

5. Are you more likely to celebrate or to criticize your differences?

6. On a scale of 1–10 (10, excellent), how are you doing?

    1___2___3___4___5___6___7___8___9___10___

7. How do you think your spouse is doing?

    1___2___3___4___5___6___7___8___9___10___

They laugh together.

Habit #6

They Laugh Often, Quickly, and Even at Themselves

They say that laughter is good for the soul. But let's put this adage into more practical terms. Not only are regular belly laughs—even a small chuckle now and then—good for the soul, researchers have found that laughter is also good for our bodies' physical well-being. There is even a science of laughter called gelotology. And the happy people who get paid to study laughter are called gelotologists.

Laughter has been found to not only help boost our immune system but to have a positive effect on circulation as well. Laughter helps to decrease anxiety and can lead to an improved mood level. There is even some evidence to suggest that laughter can help protect us from heart disease which seems reasonable since anxiety, circulation, and mood disorders have long been associated with heart disease.

All of these side benefits gained when we laugh more does not mean we should replace our next medical exam with more laughter, but if laughter has even a small positive effect on our physical and mental health, then doing more of it deserves our consideration.

Laughter can also serve us well socially since it can help create a connection between people. It can assist in building team work, cooperation, and can even play a role in diffusing defensiveness, which in turn helps accomplish conflict resolution.

Since there are benefits that laughter offers to our social, physical, and mental health and well-being, it stands to reason that regular lighthearted humor may also be good for our marriages as well. Evidence of this can be seen in observing an unhappy marriage where healthy and genuine laughter and fun is usually seldom present or altogether non-existent. On the other hand, a regular dose of genuine and appropriate laughter and lightheartedness is usually a regular occurrence in most healthy relationships.

In spite of just how important laughter is to maintaining a healthy marriage, as we grow older, it can become more difficult to spontaneously experience the fun and humor that in our youth we had with great ease and regularity. Too often, the spontaneous laughter and lighthearted experiences can be crowded out by the seriousness brought on by life events and can rob us of this very important dynamic. As time passes and the complexities of life increase (as they inevitably do), they can overshadow many of the things that at one time we found so much humorous pleasure in.

Those couples in healthy marriages know they may often have to overlook or peer beyond current difficulties that can interfere; work or no work, mortgage, disappointments, failures, kids or no kids are but a few of life events that can rob us of laughter. Then there's also world and national news as well as the inevitable aging process that can further weigh on us and short-circuit our ability to see and experience humor and laughter.

Not only do they recognize the value and importance of regular laughter, they also know that it is necessary at times to be intentional in their efforts to keep the machinery of humor well-oiled and often used. As a result, they are usually quite successful at laughing, even in the midst of these and other difficulties.

The Fine Art of Laughing at Ourselves

Laughing at ourselves occasionally is usually even more difficult than just simply laughing at things that don't directly involve us. And yet, it is ironic that most people tend to be naturally drawn to others who can do just that. We see that they feel secure enough in who they are, do not take themselves too seriously, so they are able to poke fun at themselves from time to time. Better yet, they are usually willing to take us along for the ride even when the humor is at their expense. And most of us like that in a person.

It is interesting that a characteristic often found in emotionally healthy and well-balanced children is their ability to laugh at themselves. They have somehow learned (or were they born that way?) that it is okay and even fun to frequently find humor in their own errors, mistakes, or faux pas. And most professionals who work with young children on a regular basis will agree that kids who do not take themselves too seriously and are more able to laugh at themselves typically have more friends and need to be disciplined for misbehaviors less frequently.

Letting Others Laugh at Us Too

In addition to being able to laugh at themselves, couples in healthy marriages make it a habit to actually allow the other in on the "fun at their own expense," so to speak. Just as importantly, they have both learned to first distinguish between laughing at and laughing with the other person. Of course, it is first important to determine if he/she is actually laughing at themselves before entering into the laughter. Otherwise, we just might end up laughing at, rather than with, them—seldom a good thing! Somehow, each is able to detect with regular success when their laughing in response to the blunders, imperfections, and glitches of the other is welcomed and when it is not.

Whether being able to laugh at ourselves is an innate quality or one that is learned at an early age is debatable. What we do know is that as we grow older, laughter can become less spontaneous and not as frequent. And yet, as our ability to do so is revived, it can not only improve our physical and mental health and well-being, it can also improve our marriage relationship as well.

So what's not to like about laughter?

Questions to Consider

1. Does laughter happen regularly in your relationship?

2. Has there been a change in the amount of laughter since you first met?

3. If so, what has contributed to the increase or decrease in laughter?

4. How easy/difficult is it for you to actually laugh at yourself at times?

5. Is it easy/difficult when you are the "target" of your spouse's laughter?

6. On a scale of 1–10 (10, excellent), how are you doing?

    1__2__3__4__5__6__7__8__9__10__

7. How do you think your spouse is doing?

    1__2__3__4__5__6__7__8__9__10__

Both see the importance of being vulnerable.

Habit #7

They Risk Being Vulnerable
with Each Other

There are many ways that the concept of vulnerability can be described and defined. This is my definition: "putting one's self in a position with another person who could, by taking advantage of their vulnerability, hurt them; when they don't-even though they could have-their relational and emotional intimacy increases and improves."

Fear of Being Vulnerable

Our ability and desire for vulnerable relationships seem to be a basic God-given need that all of us human beings are born with. If you doubt this, just spend a little time observing a toddler. As he learns to navigate both physically as well as relationally, he seems to be fearless; he isn't afraid of falling, doesn't seem to fear water, dogs, hot stoves, or rejection from others. And—much to the chagrin of Mom and

Dad—that little kid doesn't at first seem to fear strangers either. Early on, being vulnerable—even to a fault—seems to come quite naturally.

However, slowly but surely and through flawed relationships, imperfect life experiences, and hurtful messages from influential others, we all over time and to various degrees conclude that "this vulnerability stuff isn't at all what it's cracked up to be! I just got hurt (again!). I'd better figure out some ways to protect myself," Here are some conclusions we might have drawn as children.

- "All I wanted to do was play, and Daddy pulled the paper up in front of his face."
- "When Mommy and Daddy fight, I get yelled at."
- "All I want is for them to be proud of me. Instead, what I hear is 'If you try harder, I'm sure you can do better.'"
- "I just reached out to be close and got pushed aside because dinner was ready. I need to protect myself."
- "Mommy and Daddy stopped living together, and now I don't see Daddy very much."

The list of intimacy-busting experiences and messages that lead us to a fear of being vulnerable could go on and on. And while the severity and consistency of those messages varies dramatically from person to person, we have all experienced them and have been affected to one degree or another.

Since we all live in an imperfect world that is made up of less than perfect relationships, few are without some degree of resistance to being completely vulnerable. Few, if any of us, are willing to be as vulnerable as we were when starting out in life. Some of us are affected deeply and significantly by the hurts of the past, while fortunate others are impacted only minimally.

Just like that toddler, we have all to various degrees learned to trust less and to guard ourselves against further hurt by others. And for many, it becomes easier and safer to simply settle in to an existence of self-protection rather than to pursue a life that involves taking risks in the relationships we value most.

The Relationship between Vulnerability and Intimacy

So it is understandable that we might bring this baggage of guarding ourselves from being hurt into our marriage relationship. And since vulnerability is directly related to emotional and physical intimacy, when we avoid vulnerability, we may adversely affect the amount of intimacy we experience in our relationships.

Most couples who are struggling initially report their problem to be a decline of intimacy—the loss of the closeness, warmth, and connectedness that was present in the early days of their relationship. While the loss of intimacy is certainly problematic and must be addressed and improved, it is not the real and fundamental problem but rather, the symptom of something else going on, usually undetected and below the surface. What they initially report as "the problem," I refer to as the "symptomatic problem."

The real underlying problem below their unsatisfying level of intimacy is usually reluctance and resistance to being vulnerable in their relationship. When these fears are addressed, and they understand more about how their past experiences with vulnerability influence their current resistance, then progress in the area of intimacy can be made. Those past experiences with hurtful vulnerabilities can go way back to childhood, they can originate in prior adult relationships, or they may be from prior experiences in their current marriage relationship.

So what does it take to develop the new habit of being more vulnerable?

The key in a nutshell to overcoming the fear of vulnerability is to take the risk of stepping outside our comfort zone, in spite of the "catastrophic expectations" that we might associate with doing so. I call this effort "calling the bluff of our catastrophic expectations" and actually finding out what might happen if we allow ourselves to be in a position where the other person could hurt us (and hopefully discover that history does not repeat itself).

This risk of facing our fear and doing it anyway is really the only way to break current patterns that are usually based on painful past experiences and relationships. The hope is that as a result of doing this, we will weaken the influence our past experiences have over our present reluctance to allow ourselves to be vulnerable.

Replacing the Habit of Self-Protection with the Habit of Vulnerability

First, look back on your life experiences and relationships to better understand what may lie beneath your current resistance to being vulnerable. Does this effort take you back to any early childhood memories? Do any experiences in prior adult relationships come to mind?

- How about past experiences that occurred in your current marriage that might be blocking your ability to be as vulnerable as you would like?

- Talk together about your past and how it may be affecting your marriage. This can be a risky and vulnerable proposition in and of itself!

- Commit to challenging and supporting each other in the effort of taking more risks by stepping outside your comfort zone with each other. Understandably this will be a real challenge since doing so allows for the possibility of being hurt ("Huh? Why would I want to do that?"). Remember that there is a direct relationship between vulnerability and intimacy. That's why!

- If you are hurt as a result of your effort to be vulnerable, address it together and use it as a vehicle for growth.

- When you are trying out a new behavior of being vulnerable, let your spouse know you are in risky territory (and to please have a little mercy!).

When your efforts at being more vulnerable do not result in being hurt, then the intimacy you experience should eventually improve and your relationship is bound to grow as well.

Each time you both call the bluff of your catastrophic expectations by taking a risk and you realize the world didn't come to an end as a result, you have taken another step toward weakening an old self-defeating habit and replacing it with a new and improved one.

All easier said than done, but it *is* possible.

Questions to Consider

1. Are you able to be vulnerable in your relationship?

2. Are there areas/topics that are more difficult for you to be vulnerable in?

3. If being vulnerable is difficult, do you know why?

4. How is intimacy in your relationship affected by your ability to be vulnerable?

5. What is one risk you are willing to take in order to be more vulnerable?

6. On a scale of 1–10 (10, excellent), how are you doing?

   1___2___3___4___5___6___7___8___9___10___

7. How do you think your spouse is doing?

   1___2___3___4___5___6___7___8___9___10___

Competing for the good times seldom happens.

Habit #8

They Avoid Competing
For "the Good Times"

One common earmark of an unhealthy marriage is the habit of keeping track of the "positive life experiences" that come to the other person. Rather than a vicarious pleasure for the other, there is resentment, jealousy, and usually an attitude of indifference when good things happen to the other.

The attitude of an envious spouse who wonders when it will finally be their turn for a bit of fun, fame, or good fortune is often subtle and can even be imperceptible by others at first. Nonetheless, the one who is the focus of the resentment and envy usually knows. And it is more often than not just a matter of time until others begin to notice the subtle signs of tension developing as a result of keeping track of whose turn it is for a little fun, free time, or fifteen minutes of fame.

On the other hand, have you ever been the admiring observer of the genuine happiness and enthusiasm experienced by a spouse when good fortune has come their partner's way? Rather than resenting the good time experienced by the other, there seems to be pleasure experienced when the other is on the receiving end of something good; when one thrives or succeeds, the other seems to do so as well.

Compare the following conversations:

"Well, it looks like *you* had a very carefree and relaxing day around here while I was out slaving to make a living."

Vs.

"I'm glad you were able to take a breather today. Don't worry about what you didn't get done. You deserve a relaxing, carefree day."

*****

"Wait a minute. Do you mean to tell me that you're taking another day trip with your girl friends? When's it *my* turn?"

Vs.

"Yeah, I know you were gone not too long ago, but I'll catch up with you one of these days. Go and have a great time."

*****

"I get a little tired of hearing from others what a nice guy you are. You know, you're not exactly perfect, and they don't have to live with you."

Vs.

"I am very proud of the fact that I'm married to a person who is liked by so many people. Yeah, I know, you do have your faults, but I'm one of your fans too."

*****

"You seem to get so many comments about what a great mom you are. Don't they know it takes two to parent?"

Vs.

"I'm very proud and grateful that you are such a great mom and that your efforts don't go unnoticed by others. Our kids are lucky to have you for a mom."

*****

"Okay, so you got yet another achievement award at work this year. Don't forget that I gave up a good career of my own to stay home with the kids."

Vs.

"Your company knows a great human asset when they see one! I'm proud and thankful that you provide for us. I look forward to maybe someday jumping back into the work force myself."

Certainly not an exhaustive list of the everyday conversations that take place in marriages today, but these examples do provide a glimpse into yet another behavior and attitude habit that sets healthy marriages apart from those that are not.

It is easy for the best of us to fall into the habit of competing for positive life experiences and even resenting our spouse when they seem to be getting what we think is a little more than their fair share. But since the goal is to have a healthy and more satisfying relationship, then it is important to develop the habit of experiencing a bit of vicarious pleasure when our spouse reaps some of the rewards and benefits of life rather than resenting them and competing for them.

Questions to Consider

1.   Do you usually get pleasure from and support your spouse's good times, accolades, and successes?

2.   How does your ability/inability to do so affect your relationship?

3.   Do you feel your spouse supports and encourages you in a similar way?

4.   How does his/her ability or inability to do so affect your relationship?

5.   Do you often feel "shortchanged," or do you usually believe that the good times experienced by both tend to even out over time?

6.   On a scale of 1–10 (10, excellent), how are you doing?

   1___2___3___4___5___6__7___8___9___10___

7.   How do you think your spouse is doing?

   1___2___3___4___5___6___7___8___9___10___

They question their assumptions.

Habit #9

They Check Out Their Assumptions Before Acting on Them

Making assumptions in the process of communicating with others is inevitable, and the assumptions we make in everyday conversation are shaped and formed from the many previous experiences and relationships we have had throughout the course of our lives.

When our assumptions are correct, they serve us well; when they are incorrect (or when they are false assumptions as I will refer to them here), they can wreak havoc in our relationships. A baseball player with a batting average of .350 (one hit for three at bat for you non-baseball fans) is considered an excellent and gifted batter. When it comes to our ability to assume correctly, even a "batting average" of .900 (nine out of ten times we assume correctly) can create misunderstandings in even the best of marriages.

A few examples might help describe how our past experiences and relationships can influence our assumptions and in turn, negatively impact our responses:

A service man has just returned home from a particularly dangerous tour of duty and is enjoying a cup of coffee at an outdoor café with a friend who has been stateside establishing his accounting business. Suddenly a car going by backfires; the somewhat irritated accountant looks over at the driver and yells out, "Get your car fixed!" When he looks back at his furloughed soldier friend, he sees that he has taken cover under the table in order to protect himself from his assumed danger.

Clearly the two have had different experiences that now lead them to very different responses to the loud and disruptive sound. The accountant assumes there is a car that needs attending to and responds accordingly; the soldier, based on his recent experience in a war zone, assumes something very different and reacts based on his immediate assumption, which of course is false, that once again he is in danger. While his initial response (due to past experiences with sudden loud bangs and being shot at) is understandable, how he reacts—given his current reality—is no longer appropriate, so how he responds works against him.

Consider a husband, who as a child was constantly criticized, confronted, and mercilessly corrected on his behaviors and attitudes. And to show their displeasure, Mom and Dad would consistently withdraw from him, give him the silent treatment, and generally withhold their love for a period of time, possibly to drive home their disappointment and to manipulate him into "shaping up."

Currently, his wife challenges or in some way criticizes him (inevitable and even necessary in the best of relationships). Because of his past experiences, he falsely assumes that along with her criticism, she is also rejecting and emotionally withdrawing from him in a way similar to what he experienced with Mom and Dad.

Because he learned in childhood that criticism and emotional neglect and withdrawal go hand in hand, he reacts to his wife as if she is rejecting him, putting him down, and possibly even withdrawing her love. Yet in reality, all she has done is to challenge or maybe criticize him. And you can rest assured that the result of not checking out his assumptions will likely lead to further problems and difficulties that could have been prevented.

"When you criticize me, it brings back all sorts of memories of being rejected by Mom and Dad when they criticized me. Is that what you are doing when you criticize me?" This gives her the opportunity to clarify that although she is challenging him (maybe she is even angry at him), she in no way intends to withdraw, give him the silent treatment, or in any way respond in her displeasure the way his parents did. Yes, the process of checking out our assumptions can be somewhat laborious and time-consuming, but it beats the troubles and misunderstandings that can develop as a result of letting our false assumptions take the place of the truth.

Another example might further clarify the connection between past experiences and the assumptions we can make:

Suppose a little girl's Daddy was a consistent help around the house and that she was told that the reason he was so helpful was because he loved his family so much. This is not a bad or inappropriate message to have heard in and of itself. However, now as an adult woman, she is married to an otherwise good man who... well, let's just say that helping around the home is not exactly his strong suit.

Her need for him to be more helpful certainly is a legitimate concern and worthy of addressing. However, because she connected her dad's love for the family with his participating in household chores, she instead reacts to the false assumption that his "task-passive ways" must be a reflection of his lack of care and love for her and their family. While this is not the case, she responds emotionally as if it were, feeling unloved or unvalued—all based on the false assumption resulting from early experiences from her childhood.

In reality, the only problem is that this otherwise loving husband has a weakness in the housework category! But since her reaction is based on an early childhood message that is not necessarily true now ("Daddy helps a lot because he loves us so much"), then rather than confronting the issue of her need for more help, she responds to the false assumption that "If he really loved his family enough (the way Daddy did), he would help more."

So not only can failure to check out our assumptions before reacting lead to secondary problems, it also interferes with addressing the real and legitimate issue. In this last example, her emotional hurt based on a false assumption interfered with appropriately addressing the real problem, which was her need for more help from him around the house.

What makes checking out our assumptions difficult?

There are many possible reasons why we might resist checking out our assumptions before reacting. There are several that seem to be the most common:

- We may be unaware that there is a connection between our current assumptions and our past experiences and relationships, and it is difficult to deal effectively with current relational issues when we are unaware that there are past issues that could be interfering. Hopefully what is being suggested here will help heighten awareness and lead to a closer look at the possible connections between past experiences and relationships and your current assumptions.

- Even when we are aware of the connection between our past experiences and our current assumptions, it takes a good deal of energy, and we can just simply become a bit lazy when it comes to addressing issues. This is probably for most of us the easiest resistance to overcome when we see the importance of addressing our assumptions.

- We might be convinced that we are right in our assumptions so why bother bringing them up? Over time, this just leads to a further breakdown in communication, a deepening conviction that our assumptions are true, and that we are all the more justified in our reactions.

- "What if I find out my assumption really is correct?" When we check out our assumption, we make ourselves vulnerable; we take the risk of finding out that our assumption is in fact true (remember Habit #7: "They are willing to take the risk of being vulnerable"). "What if my assumption is correct and her criticism means she is going to withhold her love and affection as well?" "What if I am right and his refusal to be more helpful around the house really is his way of saying he doesn't care much about the family?"

It stands to reason that we could be afraid of hearing that our assumptions (our catastrophic expectations) are actually correct; it would be painful, but at least then we would have reality to deal with rather than the fears and insecurities we have held privately to ourselves.

In a healthy marriage, both make it a habit of checking out their assumptions before acting on them. If you have not yet developed this habit in your communication with each other but are willing to work at it, the results from doing so might pleasantly surprise you. You might just find that what was true in your past is no longer true in your present.

Questions to Consider

1. Do false assumptions create difficulties in your efforts to communicate?

2. If you can identify any, how are they affecting your relationship?

3. Identify a past experience that could be behind a false assumption.

4. What is a risk that makes checking out your false assumption difficult?

5. Are you willing to try checking out your assumptions before reacting?

6. On a scale of 1–10 (10, excellent), how are you doing?

   1___2___3___4___5___6___7___8___9___10___

7. How do you think your spouse is doing?

   1___2___3___4___5___6___7___8___9___10___

Neither sees the other as the bad guy.

Habit #10

They Have Learned
There Is No Room for
Good Guy-Bad Guy

Conflict now and then in just about any relationship is a given. Whether it is between siblings, business partners, teammates, or between two married people who love each other, conflict is all but inevitable. And contrary to the common belief that conflict is what destroys relationships, nothing could be further from the truth.

What weakens and undermines otherwise healthy and satisfying relationships of any kind is not the presence of conflict but rather conflict that is usually done poorly, destructively, and for the wrong motivation.

Conflict and disagreement that carry with them the attitude and desire of making the other guy the "bad" guy in order to come out on top seldom leads to a healthy resolution. In contrast to a mutually satisfactory outcome, when personal attack takes over, the conflict resembles a tug-of-war, where there is a mean and hungry alligator in the middle just waiting for the weaker combatant to fall in. If a participant in the conflict wants to avoid being eaten (an understandable avoidance), their survival instincts must kick in. When this happens the only alternative to being defeated is to defeat, and the typical weapons of choice are usually personal jabs and hurtful comments.

Unfortunately, when our goals in the conflict shift from solving the problem to surviving, our efforts become motivated by our need to win in order to avoid losing. And when this shift in goals happens, it is easier to resort to destructive responses such as "That's the most ridiculous thing I've ever heard," "Where did you come up with such a dumb idea?" "Give me a break!" "You're sounding more like your mother now!" Most would no doubt agree that all are various forms of putdowns and dismissive responses that yield nothing productive for anyone.

In a healthy relationship, both make it a habit of agreeing to do their best to avoid words, looks, gestures, and attitudes—spoken or otherwise—that might accuse the other person of being "the problem." And they agree they will instead do their best to see the conflict as the real culprit. Few do this perfectly, but success doesn't require perfection. But when both are reasonably successful in their efforts, it is easier for both to stay on track, rather than on the attack.

When you stop to think about it, when we resort to personal attacks and putdowns in an effort to win, isn't it likely that in the long run both will be negatively affected? When either ends up branded the bad guy, there will be inevitable side effects that show up in other areas of our relationship. When we make the other guy the bad guy in order to come out the victor in a conflict through the use of putdowns, the bond that is designed to hold us together is damaged and weakened in the process.

Labeling our opponent, the bad guy, in order to ramp up our combative skills and our determination to win the conflict may be okay and actually work to our advantage in sports, world wars, and fist fights. But our efforts to have our way with our spouse by doing so can undermine what it takes to build and maintain a healthy and satisfying marriage relationship.

A more reasonable and satisfying habit found in healthy marriages is the mutual determination to somehow get themselves on the same side in order to more successfully work together and against what they agree is their mutual problem. They both recognize and agree that the other is not the "enemy," the problem or the bad guy and that the real culprit is the conflict that threatens to divide and conquer their relationship.

Being on the same side working against the common problem or conflict certainly does not rule out the possibility of anger, frustration, or a whole host of other emotions in the midst of cooperatively working through the common conflict. It simply means that each one exerts whatever effort needed to avoid viewing the other as "the enemy" or as one who must be defeated in order to resolve the conflict.

This is what the habit of being on the same side working against the common problem looks like:

- neither is arguing for the sake of arguing, since both feel strongly about their position;

- believing that he/she is no more "the problem" than you are;

- rejecting the notion that if the other would just give in, then problem solved;

- an acceptance that the needs and opinions of the other are just as important as yours; agreeing with them is not required;

- believing that the motivation of the other is not to defeat you;

- understanding that personal attacks do not work to get what you want;

- understanding that if you win by attacking personally, then you have defeated your spouse ("Do you really want to live with someone who has been defeated?");

- committing to the idea that regardless of how heated the issue, neither will resort to personal attacks

All of these conditions take a healthy dose of humility and an acceptance that "I'm not the only one living on this island." Remember, someone else washed on to shore the day you were married.

When we are in the habit of using personal attacks to get our way and to avoid being defeated, then building and maintaining a healthy marriage becomes a far more difficult task to achieve. On the other hand, when we make it a habit to work toward getting ourselves on the same side in order to solve the mutual problem, then we have strengthened the bond between us and helped create a healthier, more satisfying relationship.

Once again, easier said than done, but it *is* possible!

Questions to Consider

1. Does "good guy-bad guy" attitude ever enter into your relationship?

2. If it does, how does it interfere with your ability to resolve issues?

3. What is a personal attack that come with good guy-bad guy?

4. Have you ever resolved an issue with personal attacks?

5. What long term damage occurs when good guy-bad guy is used?

6. On a scale of 1–10 (10, excellent), how are you doing?

    1___2___3___4___5___6___7___8___9___10___

7. How do you think your spouse is doing?

    1___2___3___4___5___6___7___8___9___10___

Solving the problem together is their goal.

Habit #11

They Want to Solve the Problem Rather than Win the Battle

At first glance, there may seem to be little difference between this healthy habit of solving the problem rather than winning the battle and #10—the habit of avoiding the "good guy-bad guy" mind set. While the two are similar in some ways, there are a few important distinctions.

For instance, it is possible to successfully avoid the "good guy-bad guy" habit that can derail efforts to successfully resolve a conflict while at the same time still be motivated by one's own personal need to win rather than to resolve. Both can successfully avoid the putdowns and personal attacks that make up the good guy-bad guy battle tactic addressed in #10 but still be more focused on winning the battle and getting what they want rather than the compromise that is needed to solve the problem at hand.

So in addition to avoiding the good guy-bad guy mentality, couples in a healthy marriage also make it a habit to resist being motivated by their own need to win when they conflict. As a result of eliminating—or at least minimizing—their need to win, they are more likely to successfully work toward resolving the conflict; competition is replaced with cooperation.

In a "win-lose," winner take all conflict—even when dirty tactics are absent—striving to win still requires beating the person competing against our satisfaction. Yet in a marriage where there is this kind of competition, to declare ourselves the winner is to declare our spouse the loser; since we have won, they have lost, and it is at their expense that we are able to claim victory (any idea what it's like to live with a person who is defeated? It's not a pretty picture!).

It is natural for most of us to think first about winning rather than solving the problem when there is a conflict between ourselves and another. The assumption is that "if I am somehow able to pull off a win, well then, problem solved." While that might hold true in some circumstances with others where there is a conflict or disagreement, when it comes to marriage relationships, it doesn't seem to go all that well. And yet it is easy for our first thought to be about how we can win rather than the goal of solving the problem to the benefit of both.

We set the stage for solving the mutual problem and both surviving the conflict, when as in #10, we not only avoid making the other guy the bad guy, but we acknowledge that the needs and opinions of the other are every bit as important as our own. This does not require that either entirely sacrifices their needs for those of the other (although once in a while, doing so might not be such a bad idea!) or that their differing views must eventually match up. It does, however, call for taking into very serious consideration the needs and opinions of the other. When the focus is first on our own needs, our consideration of the other's tends to blur.

Solving the problem and surviving the conflict requires that we learn to trust that the other is not motivated in their efforts by a need to control or to win for the sake of their pride, that he/she is not conflicting simply for the sake of winning. Rather, we trust that their opposing position really is a reflection of their belief, conviction, need, or opinion. Solving the conflict rather than fighting to win the battle takes recognizing that it is not necessary to win in order to avoid losing and keeping in mind that the conflict isn't about winning or losing, but about resolving the issue and then peacefully moving on together.

Finally, in order to avoid the temptation of conflicting for the sake of winning the battle, it helps to remember that if you win, then your spouse has lost. (Remind me again what life is like living with someone who feels like they have been defeated?) And it is important to note once again that working toward a healthy marriage does not call for eliminating conflict altogether but rather the habit of doing the conflict well. When conflicts are addressed constructively, many other potentially destructive issues are avoided, since so often one unresolved and messy conflict becomes the foundation for the next...and the next...and the next...

Questions to Consider

1. In your relationship, is winning vs. losing a part of your conflicts?

2. If winning vs. losing is the motivation, what's it like for you when you have gotten the best of your spouse (if you win, he/she loses)?

3. When winning vs. losing motivates your efforts, what's it like when your spouse has gotten the best of you (when your spouse wins, you lose)?

4. If you have ever experienced solving a conflict together rather than setting out to win, what was that experience like for you?

5. Does the notion that you must win in order to avoid losing ever motivate either of you to win?

6. On a scale of 1–10 (10, excellent), how are you doing?

   1___2___3___4___5___6___7___8___9___10___

7. How do you think your spouse is doing?

   1___2___3___4___5___6___7___8___9___10___

They understand the importance
of avoiding regrets.

Habit #12

They Treat Each Other as
if Today Were Their Last

O kay. A bit morose, but it needs to be said. Here goes!
    Not too long ago, I suggested this notion to a friend that we
    should all treat our spouses as if this were the last day we would
be together. He was not exactly impressed with the wisdom of such an
idea. "If I thought that today was our last day on earth together," he
retorted, "I would literally not leave her side. It would not only be impossible to do that every day, but that would be no way to live our lives."

Fair enough. This is true. But in taking my suggestion to an
extreme, my friend missed the point. To his credit, in further discussion with him, he conceded that if he knew they were living their last
day together, it would definitely have a profound effect on his words,
attitudes, and behaviors.

So how does our relationship benefit when we make it a habit to
treat our spouse as if today were our last day together? Two benefits

come to mind. One has to do with regret, the other with positive memories.

When we are reminded of this uncertainty, it can help us live in such a way that will help minimize the possibility of future regrets. Granted, since to be human is to be hopelessly imperfect, it is inevitable that we will have some regrets that we will have to deal with at the end of our time together. But our greatest and most painful regrets will not be over the mistakes we've made that were followed with the opportunity to reconcile. The most painful regrets will be the ones we no longer have the opportunity to resolve and reconcile. (I warned you this one would be a bit morose!)

Fortunately, when we are granted another day with our spouse, we are given the opportunity to revisit our misdeed, apologize, reconcile, and then move on together. Since we are given another day to repair our misdeed, we are able to dilute or even eliminate altogether the regret factor.

On the other hand, if the opportunity to reconcile were taken from us because yesterday was our last (we just didn't know it!), the resulting regrets created because we can only wish we could take back our actions are hard to resolve and get beyond. We all know this is true at some level, but it is important to remind ourselves from time to time (maybe daily!) since it is easy for us to live as if "there's always another day."

Probably there will be; hopefully so. But what if there weren't?

There is another benefit that comes with the habit of living as if today were the last day with our spouse. This habit that most successful marriages consistently embrace also helps to consistently maintain the attitudes and behaviors that help build and strengthen their relationship.

So this habit not only discourages behaviors and attitudes that will someday—when it is too late—be regrettable, but it also provides us with the motivation to be more intentional in acting in the positive ways that bring about not only a deeper and more satisfying relationship but positive memories to someday look back on.

Questions to Consider

1. Are there any ways you act, behave, or communicate that if today were your spouse's last, you would regret?

2. Would living today as if this were your spouse's last, make a difference in any of your attitudes/behaviors/words?

3. What would you eliminate and what positive would you replace it with?

4. In what ways would your relationship benefit if you treated your spouse as if this were your last day together?

5. Would your spouse behave differently if he/she made this a habit?

6. On a scale of 1–10 (10, excellent), how are you doing?

   1___2___3___4___5___6___7___8___9___10___

7. How do you think your spouse is doing?

   1___2___3___4___5___6___7___8___9___10___

They are aware of the baggage they bring.

Habit #13

They Are Aware of the Baggage They Bring to Their Relationship

t is a common false assumption that our previous life experiences—whether from childhood or from our earlier adult years—are "water under the bridge" and consequently irrelevant to our "current life pattern." Nothing could be further from the truth. Our past experiences and relationships do play a significant role, and depending on our ability to overcome their influences, they can determine the success or failure of not only our marriage relationship but other relationships as well.

Where Does the Baggage We Bring into Our Marriage Come from?

Our past life experiences, relationships, and messages from others can significantly influence what our current life pattern looks like. Depending on what our childhood experiences were, they can either lead to painful and destructive life patterns, or they may have the potential of providing a healthy and positive influence. For most of us, we bring a combination of both.

Since we live in an imperfect world with imperfect people, it is all but certain that we enter our marriage relationship with some baggage and its potential influence. The good news is that we are not inevitably held captive by either the mistakes others have made or the painful experiences we may have endured. Our potential freedom from our past can be gained through writing a new script and making new decisions by challenging any painful or misguided messages we might have heard during our early years.

It is difficult to overstate just how powerful the influences—both positive and negative—were that others had on us when we were young. Unlike our adult brain, when we were young and just starting out in life, it responded more like a sponge, absorbing without being able to question what it was told, what it observed, and what it experienced. Our original sponge-like brain was not yet able to think for itself; it just absorbed. Basically, our responses were "So *that's* who I am! So *that's* what/how they expect me to be! So *that's* what I have to offer!" Our early childhood influences then became a "road map" of sorts, shaping and directing so much of what lay ahead.

"Brainwashing" And the Role It Plays in Our Current Life Patterns

Have you ever wondered why it is that you call a "couch," a couch; why you have labeled a "light bulb," a light bulb? What influenced you to refer to a "horse" as a horse? That's what you were told over and over again, and each time, your little sponge-like brain responded, "So *that's* what that is! It's a couch/light bulb/horse!" Yes, you were taught to blindly label these and other objects, and that was a good and proper use of brainwashing.

This influence I refer to as early childhood brainwashing (you may prefer another term like shaping or influencing, but I'm sticking with brainwashing) might have been used in a healthy and productive way and with good intentions like giving us expectations to live *up* to, or it might have worked to our disadvantage by giving us expectations to live *down* to. So both healthy as well as unhealthy brainwashing shaped and influenced our personality since, as we grew and matured, we had the tendency to set out in life, fulfilling and substantiating what we were originally told about ourselves. For instance:

- a little boy who is consistently told by Mom and Dad that he is polite and that they like that in a person;
  likely results: he will grow up living up to that feedback, treating others with respect;

- when the message is loud, clear, and consistent that he is fun to be with;
  likely results: he will grow up to be, well, a fun person to be around;

- when told regularly that she is a good friend to others;
  likely results: she will grow up being just that—a friend who can be counted on;

- kids who grow up being challenged when necessary but without being degraded and belittled;
  likely results: they likely grow up being able to take challenges from others without disrupting their relationship or bruising their self-esteem.

Or the childhood messages and expectations heard from others can work against us and lead to self-defeating baggage that can be carried into our marriage as well as into other relationships. For instance:

- growing up being the family scapegoat, blamed for just about anything that went wrong;
  likely results: as an adult, being convinced that "when anything goes wrong, it must be my fault" ("I guess that's my role"). Or perhaps the opposite result—refusing to take responsibility for anything that goes wrong ("I'm tired of being blamed, and it isn't going to happen any longer");

- growing up being excessively controlled;
  likely results: they may either become easily and inappropriately controlled ("I guess that's my role") or perhaps the opposite—refusing to be controlled in any way, even when it is appropriate ("I'm tired of being controlled, and it isn't going to happen any longer");

- maybe the early childhood message was that men (women) are not to be trusted;
  likely results: they grow up having difficulty trusting.

- the baggage of personal insecurity as a result of a childhood filled with putdowns, criticisms, and accusations;
likely results: a spouse who expects his/her partner to constantly build him/her up but seldom really believing their attempts are sincere.

- the baggage of abandonment as a result of distant, unavailable, or physically absent parents;
likely results: a spouse who unreasonably insists on their partner being present or at least, available; smothering, demanding, and suspiciousness are standard characteristics of a spouse who still believes that being abandoned by the one she loves is right around the corner and thus must not let their spouse out of their sight any more than necessary. ("I am more 'leave-able' than I am lovable.")

- the baggage of what I call "conflict connection," typically the result of growing up in a family where constant fighting, bickering, and conflicting was the norm and most common form of connecting with each other.
likely results: the ability to connect only by way of conflict. "Negative strokes are better than no strokes at all" is the unconscious cry of those who have a history of conflict connection. Because of the innate need to connect with others, the habit of connecting via conflict becomes not only the norm but seen as the only possible way of connecting with others.

So Am I Stuck with the Effects of My Baggage?

We need not look any further than the incredible transformation that occurred in the life of Derek Black, as an encouraging example of how we are not inevitably held captive by our early childhood influences.

Derek's father was a prominent white Nationalist leader who was grooming his son to follow in his footsteps. Derek's godfather was none other than David Duke, a Grand Wizard in the KKK Nationalist movement.

By the end of his teen years, Derek was himself a leader in the Nationalist movement whose goal it was to "take the country back" by purging the United States of "inferior" race—basically all races that were not white.

To summarize his long and transformative journey, the beginning of his coming to new conclusions was the result of an orthodox Jew, inviting him to a Shabbat dinner. It was there that he began to question what he had been told—the bill of goods he had been sold—and the negative and hateful brainwashing he had undergone his entire life. Slowly but surely, he began the process of questioning all of the white supremacist beliefs and doctrines he had been brainwashed to believe as "the truth."

In time, Derek not only completely disavowed what he had been taught during his formative years about white supremacy, but he has become a spokesman against the very movement he had been groomed to lead.

There is no better example of how we do not have to be held captive by any of the negative influences that otherwise have a negative hold on our current life pattern.

It's not a question of whether or not we have baggage—we all have baggage. I suppose that's why Woody Allen once referred to all of us human beings as "normal neurotics." While we can't just push the delete button and eliminate our past influences, it is possible to have a significant say over how those past events, relationships, messages, and observations influence our current life pattern.

So the goal is not to ignore or deny our baggage, or even fret over the fact that we, like everyone else, have it. Rather a more doable goal is to be in control of it and to recognize that we no longer must be held captive by negative and self-defeating thoughts from the past and that our past not only does not have to repeat itself, it no longer must inevitably dictate how we conduct ourselves in our current relationships, just as Derek Black took control over his past hateful influences.

There is no simple recipe for overcoming the influences from our past, and it is usually no easy task to do so. But it is possible, and the following might provide a bit of a kickstart to the process:

- Be more *aware* of any past experiences, messages, and observations—the good, the bad, and the ugly—that may be interfering with how you would like your life/marriage to be today.
- Work to *understand* what conclusions or decisions you might have come to about yourself and the rest of the world as a result of the messages you heard and the observations you made.
- Take *responsibility* for how you currently allow those influences to shape your thoughts and behaviors.
- Work to *replace* any childhood roadmaps that negatively affect your current life pattern. By all means, keep the good messages and work toward eliminating the bad ones.
- Make new *decisions*. You are who you are not so much because of the mistakes others have made but rather, how you have chosen—decided—over the years to respond to their mistakes. This is good news because it means you potentially have the power and ability to make new and more productive decisions.

We do not have to continue being held captive by the past and the mistakes others have made with us. Nor must we remain a victim of those mistakes.

Our road map, by the way, *can* be changed!

Questions to Consider

1. What baggage from your past experiences and relationships do you come into your marriage with?

2. Are there ways that your baggage affects your current life pattern and specifically your marriage?

3. To what degree are you able to control how your baggage affects your relationship?

4. Are you and your spouse able to talk about the baggage you both bring?

5. What risk, if any, is there in talking with your spouse about your baggage, or do you feel safe in doing so?

6. On a scale of 1–10 (10, excellent), how are you doing?

    1___2___3___4___5___6___7___8___9___10___

7. How do you think your spouse is doing?

    1___2___3___4__-5___6___7___8___9___10___

They value and respect the needs of the other.

Habit #14

They Consistently Consider Putting Their Spouse's Needs Ahead of Their Own

Consistently considering the needs of the other is a habit often found in healthy marriages, but it is important to emphasize that this habit does not suggest or require that they must always place their needs ahead of their own. "Consistently consider" are the operative words here that are found in healthy relationships. It does stand to reason, however, that when they genuinely consider the needs of the other, choosing to honor their spouse's over their own will happen from time to time.

In this world where "it's every man for himself" is too often the mindset, it is refreshing when occasionally we are witness to a relationship that actually operates in a more selfless and yet mutually satisfying manner.

I was fortunate to have had a model of this alternative way of being in a relationship. Both my mother and father-in-law were that model (and if you are thinking that must have been a hard act to follow, you're right!). And I would have to say that due in large part to their consistently looking out for the needs of the other, they had a near perfect marriage (actually perfect marriage, but I wouldn't expect anyone to really believe that claim!).

Joan and I were young in our marriage, and I was just starting out in private practice, so I was eager to hear from some real experts in the field of marriage relationships how they made it work. One day, I asked them both separately and privately what the one thing would be that they could give credit to for their very healthy and vibrant marriage.

First, I asked Jim. After pausing to think through his response, he said this:

"I think what's most important to me is what's important to Dorothy."

Then I tracked down Dorothy and asked her the same question. Similar to Jim, she paused. Then she said this: "What's most important to me is what's important to Jim."

Jim and Dorothy both consistently considered placing before their own wants and desires those of the other. Neither was a door mat, neither would say they went without much, and both were very happy, satisfied, and appreciative people. Rather than focusing so much on what they needed and wanted from the relationship, they both focused more on what they could contribute to the other.

Sacrificial? No, not really. They both came out ahead.

A dull and uneventful relationship? Hardly.

A doormat relationship? No. Since they shared the same perspective, their relationship was symbiotic rather than parasitic.

Jim and Dorothy both put their appreciation and value for their relationship ahead of their own individual needs. It was not as though they didn't have needs, but the needs they had seemed seldom to be as important as the needs of the other. Since they were both willing and able to consistently adhere to this value, neither missed out on much, if anything. Granted, if only one had seen the value of this other-centered kind of marriage, it would not have worked. Instead, theirs would have been a parasitic, doormat kind of relationship.

Marriages that adopt this habit of seriously taking into consideration the needs of the other really do end up sacrificing very little since, while one is looking out for the needs of the other, the other person is doing the same. If I ever saw Jim and Dorothy quibble over anything, it was over who was going to set their need and desire aside for the sake and satisfaction of the other.

I am the first to say—and I say it from experience—easier said than done. Few are able to pull this habit off with perfection but striving to do so is the goal that can make a difference.

And it is worth emphasizing once again that this kind of self-lessness works in a marriage only when it is the mutual vision and goal of both. If only one makes this standard a regular consideration, then what develops is a doormat, enabling relationship. While this one-sided arrangement leads to a "give-and-take" relationship, it is the "you give, I take" kind of marriage that doesn't work well.

One benefit that is pumped into a relationship when we endeavor to accomplish this daunting task of considering the needs of the other before our own is the elimination of unhealthy and unnecessary competition. We minimize the win-lose attitude, and we actually may even experience a vicarious satisfaction via the satisfaction of the other.

Since the results of this habit are in the long run mutually beneficial, then deferring to the needs of the other feels a bit more palatable. After all, in such a relationship where both are looking out for the other, both are confident in knowing that it is just a matter of time until the same is offered back. Both are more satisfied than they would have been if they had to compete to get their way over their spouse's.

If we could rid our relationship of selfishness and replace it with a bit more selflessness (admittedly an altogether impossible task), then we would also eliminate many of the secondary "problems" that are symptomatic of the underlying cancer of selfishness. While the notion that we might be able to perfect this healthy habit is fool-hardy, simply coming closer through our efforts would be a good start and might just make a real difference.

Questions to Consider

1. Does your spouse consider your needs as much as you would like?

2. Do you regularly consider your spouse's needs?

3. Growing up, what was your model for considering the needs of the other?

4. What was your spouse's model for considering the needs of the other?

5. If you both were to consider more the needs of the other, how do you think your marriage would be affected?

6. On a scale of 1–10 (10, excellent), how are you doing with this habit?

   1___2___3___4___5___6___7___8___9___10___

7. How do you think your spouse is doing?

   1___2___3___4___5___6___7___8___9___10___

Both are proud of the other—and they say so once in a while.

Habit #15

They Look for the Opportunity to Brag Just A Bit about Their Spouse

We've all been at parties and other events where we were held captive by and subjected to a braggadocio spouse reporting on all the life-long successes of their partner. We found ourselves daydreaming, wondering if it would ever end, and thinking, "Do I really even care about all their accomplishments?"

This kind of braggadocio is what gives bragging a bad name, and that's not what we're encouraging here. While it might be wise to spare our audience all the details, the habit of occasionally commenting to others on how proud and thankful we are of our spouse can have a number of benefits and add petrol to our relationship. Not to mention the fact that it's just the right thing to do.

Is there a difference between complimenting and bragging?

While both are beneficial to our relationship, there is a simple but important difference between the two:

Complimenting is the act of privately telling your spouse what you like about them, what you are drawn to, and what you appreciate about them—certainly a characteristic found in healthy relationships.

Bragging, on the other hand, is going public with your compliment; it is the act of occasionally and briefly commenting to others what you like and appreciate about your spouse. Typically, complementing comes easier than bragging since we may fear that going public with our compliments will be seen as being self-serving and braggadocio.

Have you ever noticed the response of a young child who has been acknowledged for a task well done or for a successful accomplishment? They usually light up with a smile of pride, having had their efforts acknowledged. And when they are complimented in the presence of others (bragged on briefly just a bit), the benefits are even greater since "the whole world knows about my success, and that feels good!" And as we have suggested earlier, the recognition of having done a good job—either by private feedback or publicly—serves as a motivation to keep up the good work. Clearly the recognition warms their heart, and their confidence is given an extra boost because they have been recognized.

Perhaps it could be said that as we grow older, we may to some degree outgrow our need for recognition and that a little praise as an adult goes a longer way than it did when we were a kid. But most of us do still light up (if only privately) when we are recognized, whether privately or better yet, in public once in a while. Most of us are just not willing to admit how important both private and public recognition is.

What prevents our being more privately as well as publicly complimentary?

Far too often, there seems to be what I refer to as "an economy on compliments." By that I mean, the baseless and false assumption that we have been given just a certain number of compliments that we are able to give out over the course of our lifetime, so we'd better distribute them sparingly. We must not go overboard, or we might run out of the allotment we have been given. In spite of the absurdity of such an idea, I do believe there is at least a bit of this unconscious mindset that influences our tendency to be miserly when it comes to doling out either private or public compliments.

Another unfortunate deterrent to occasionally bragging a bit about our spouse is that it can feel like we are bragging about ourselves. This can certainly be an accurate perception of others if we go on and on (and on and on and on...) rather than keeping our positive comments closer to the length of a sound bite.

There may be the concern that too much recognition could result in a swelled head on the part of our spouse. Go ahead and take that risk; if it happens, then deal with it.

It may be that holding back on compliments is a form of revenge for not getting enough ourselves. While this may indeed be the case, there are better ways of addressing our need for more positive feedback.

Our spouse may be, well, dragging their feet a bit and not measuring up in other ways. It is easy then to withhold our compliments where they deserve them, if they are letting us down in other areas.

Aside from the fact that it is just simply the right thing to do, there are benefits that result in complimenting (bragging) on our spouse from time to time. The most obvious and possibly greatest of all is the message it sends to our spouse. Our efforts to let them know what we like and value about them goes a long way in building and supporting their self-esteem.

And there is an added message we send when we go public with our accolades—that we want others to know just how proud of them we are. This effort injects even more good will and significance into our relationship. When describing their need to be acknowledged— both privately and occasionally in public—women typically use the word *cherished*, while men usually refer to being valued or feeling relevant. Both men and women need more of both.

And then there is the message we send to our kids when we compliment their other parent. When we occasionally brag on our spouse in their presence, we provide a model for them to follow in not only their current but future relationships as well. They learn that complimenting makes others feel good.

Yet another benefit that comes from the habit of privately and publicly complimenting our spouse is that it can crowd out and leave less room for complaining. When we verbalize genuinely positive thoughts, we tend to have a better perspective on whatever negative might also be present in our relationship. It's too often easier to criticize than it is to compliment, and it can be even more so common in our relationship with the one we are supposed to love and honor the most.

And how about the possible benefit that others may be influenced and as a result, add to their relationship the new habit of occasionally bragging about their spouse a bit? What we model can have a profound influence on others.

So it is important to intentionally work toward and strengthen the good habit of complimenting our spouse both privately as well as publicly, i.e., bragging to others just a bit about them. In addition to the fact that it is simply the right thing to do, the benefits will likely over time begin to show up in the form of a healthier and more fulfilling relationship.

Isn't that what we all really want?

Questions to Consider

1. Does bragging on your spouse now and then come naturally to you?

2. If you have a hard time going public with your compliments, do you know why?

3. Does your spouse compliment you publicly from time to time?

4. If/when your spouse compliments you publicly, how does that make you feel?

5. How might your relationship improve if there were more public compliments taking place?

6. On a scale of 1–10 (10, excellent), how are you doing with this habit?

    1___2___3___4___5___6___7___8___9___10___

7. How do you think your spouse is doing?

    1___2___3___4___5___6___7___8___9___10___

They still have fun together.

Habit #16

They Make It a Priority to Have Fun Together

A re we still having fun?

Show me a happy and successful married couple, and I will show you two people who still know how to have fun. I say "still" since in the beginning, didn't most of us start out having fun together? In fact, most relationships usually start off having nothing but fun! It kind of begs the question: what happened to all the fun we started out having together?

I'll tell you what happened—work, mortgage, more work to pay the mortgage, the toilet seat constantly left up, lights unnecessarily left on, more work to pay the light bill, employment, unemployment, errands, household chores. All of these real-life circumstances and more do inevitably kick in. And when they do, they can chip away at what once was a fun-loving, devil-may-care relationship, leaving in its place a marriage that is at times more heavy and drab than it is fun.

Oh, and did I mention kids? Discipline, babysitters, more work to pay for the babysitters, medical bills, tutoring, sport schedule and expenses—lots more reality we could add to this list of potential fun busters, but I will stop before we all become even more overwhelmed!

At first glance, this may sound fatalistically bleak and hopeless. But there is hope. True, all the above life events do happen, and with each one, we can lose the ability to experience the spontaneous fun we had in the beginning of our friendship. After all, in those early days of our relationship, we may not have had much money, but we usually had more time and the freedom to be spontaneous. And regardless of what we chose to do together, it was fun since it was with this new and exciting person we were getting to know.

No mortgage, no toilet seat left up. And if it were left up, it didn't matter since our newly found passion transcended any minor irritation over a silly toilet seat. No problem with lights left on since the utilities were covered in our renal agreement. And even if they weren't, it didn't matter since our newly found passion rendered us blind to such minor transgressions.

By now, you no doubt get my drift; when the reality of living together and all that comes with it kicks in, life inevitably becomes more complicated, and with it all, the early fun that came so naturally and with great regularity becomes harder to come by.

But the prospect of still having fun together in the midst of all the complications is still possible. The hope is found when we realize that fun can still be had by all but that it may now take more effort and more energy to replace the fading spontaneity that was once present before all the complexities of life came flooding in.

The New Ingredient Required: Intentionality

A University of Denver research project in 2008 found that the more fun couples had together, the happier and more satisfying they reported their marriages to be. While this study shows the significant relationship between having fun together and the level of happiness and satisfaction, it does not address the importance of being intentional in our efforts in order to keep the fun alive.

While not the result of an official study, my observations have led me to conclude that couples who are still having fun—whether they have been married six months or sixty years—are able to do so as a result of intentionally exerting the greater effort that becomes necessary as real life kicks in.

They recognize the importance of planning ahead together in order to make room for the fun times; they recognize the necessity of occasionally going out and doing something fun or entertaining, even though they may not always feel like doing so.

They understand that although they seldom had to look ahead and plan for the fun times early in their relationship, they do now. And they have probably agreed together not to easily cave into the weariness that comes with not only age but the responsibility of dealing with the newly acquired stressors that were somehow not there in the beginning.

A friend recently commented that they were told at a retirement seminar that there are three stages that retired folk go through: there's the "go-go" period where they are feeling their new-found freedom from work and now are going to go and do more. Then according to the retirement experts, there's the "slow-go" period where they slow down just a bit, followed by the "no-go" stage where, well, that period is self-explanatory.

While I suppose for all of us, the no-go stage will eventually come, couples in healthy relationships seem to put it off as long as possible.

So what does having fun look like?

A good question, but just as "beauty is in the eye of the beholder," so too is having fun together in the eye of the beholders. So the answer will vary depending on who you ask. There is no master list that works universally for everyone; one man's fun is another's drudgery. But here are a few suggestions to get you started:

- Find things to joke about, to laugh at together.
- Share your own goof-ups and laugh over them together;
- Share funny stories or videos you come across on the internet;

- Find the humor in some of the things your kids do that are a bit off the wall;
- Plan ahead to go out to dinner or a movie together;
- Find ways to be more playful with each other;
- Talk together about what was fun for you both when you first met. Consider revisiting some of them now;
- Plan and prepare meals together on a regular basis
- Take a class that is of interest to you both
- If funds are tight—even if they aren't—go to free community events/activities;
- Take a night away somewhere fun or meaningful to you both;
- Make a certain day(s) each month a date night. Take turns planning;
- Identify a couple that appeals to you both and initiate with them;
- Find a couple you trust and take turns swapping kids for a night out;
- If you have kids, include them some and even ask them to plan an activity;
- Take a walk together and agree not to talk about work or others;
- Sit on a bench downtown and observe people together;
- Take in a sunset (or a sunrise might work just as well);
- Volunteer together and talk about the experience.
- And finally, make your own list of the things you think would be fun, and then follow through and do them.

So the message here is simple, and it is this: there is still plenty of fun to be had as you and your relationship inevitably age, but it will likely take more intentionality to make it happen.

So what's not to like about having fun?

Questions to Consider

1. Are you still in the habit of having fun together?

2. If so, does it still come as naturally, or does it take more effort now?

3. If not, what current life events interfere with the fun you once had?

4. What would being more intentional in your effort to have fun look like?

5. If you were to have more fun, how would it benefit your relationship?

6. On a scale of 1–10 (10, excellent), how are you doing with this habit?

   1___2___3___4___5___6___7___8___9___10___

7. How do you think your spouse is doing?

   1___2___3___4___5___6___7___8___9___10___

They communicate well together.

Habit #17

They Hear the Heart of the Other, Not Just Their Words

Philosophers for years have asked and debated the question, "When a tree falls in the wilderness, and there is no one around to hear, does the falling tree make a noise?"

Either I am not smart enough, or maybe I just don't care to come up with a reasonable opinion on the subject, let alone enter into a debate with the wiser and learned scholars who contemplate such thoughts. What I do know and can say for sure is this: when someone talks, and no one is listening, then communication has not occurred; when words are heard, but the heart of the one speaking is not, then little has been communicated. This is the way it is in many struggling relationships.

A Common Communication Difference
Between Men and Women

When asked to describe what communication is like in their relationship, there is often a rather consistent difference in how men describe their experience compared to how women do. The pattern of communication may vary a bit from couple to couple, but generally, men report that when their wife is talking, she will often "go on and on" and tends to repeat herself. And usually, "She's talking about her *feelings!*" (And it's a no-brainer to assume that most men would rather be talking about sports, beer, or power tools!) And since she gets the feeling that he is really not getting what she is saying, she continues to talk, hoping to finally connect. She may package her words a bit differently each time, but what he hears is basically the same message repeated multiple ways and multiple times. In response, he daydreams even more and retreats further into his own world.

Women, on the other hand, tend to view the communication process with their husbands differently (so what else is new?). Many report that they usually do all the talking in a conversation, and their husband just sits there, looking bored and disinterested, and often they are; their communication takes the form of a monologue rather than the dialogue they would like. While this may not be a universal pattern, it is reported regularly enough to be a problem in lots of marriages.

When women do not receive the verbal and nonverbal response that show they are really being heard, they are more likely to repeat themselves, thinking that somehow packaging their message in a different way might finally get a response and lead to a connection.

Instead of getting the signs from him that show she is being heard, he checks out even further since she is repeating herself. He then privately turns his attention to things that to him are more pressing and interesting issues—golf, the account at work that is falling through, whether or not they really need that new power tool, whether they will have time before work to swing by for a latte, if he will be able to cover this month's mortgage, and "How 'bout them

Dodgers?" You name it, and his mind goes there—anywhere but the here and now and the repetitious droning of his wife.

And the repetitive cycle continues and repeats itself the next time.

A New and Healthier Communication Habit

In a healthy marriage, he has figured out that she wants both her voice and her heart to be heard rather than simply be passively listened to and then dismissed. He makes it a habit to really listen and to do his part in having a dialogue, even if at times the conversation is about things that may not be that important to him. Somewhere along the line, he realizes that he needs to develop some communication skills that will send the message to his wife that not only is he hearing her voice but that he is actually hearing her heart.

So here is a short course in communication:

Acceptance: Showing acceptance is not necessarily a sign that you agree. Simply an occasional and strategically placed "Hmm, really?" or an occasional nod of the head that conveys you're with her. And don't forget the eye contact (but then that means you'll have to actually put down that darn hand-held device!).

Reflection: Regularly saying back in new and fresh words what you think you heard her say "sounds like you really had fun," or "that took some guts to tell her that!"

Clarification: Used when you are not clear about what she is saying. "I'm not sure I get that last part. Could you help me understand what you just said?" Or "Before you go any further, what did you mean when you said your new friend is a bit 'sketchy'?" Simply stated, when we ask for clarification, we show our interest in what is being said.

Interpretation: Use it sparingly, but occasionally risk reading between the lines of what you think you hear her saying. It is useful in showing you are involved with what she is telling you. "You aren't actually saying this, but it sounds like you don't have much time for or interest in your new class." Or "Correct me if I'm wrong, but do you think maybe what you are really afraid of is that you might not do so well in the class?"

Summary: Used at the end of a conversation to sum up briefly what you talked about. It's not always necessary and can even seem a bit laborious so pass on this one when it doesn't fit.

Just writing and explaining the finer points of good communication makes me tired (I have to admit, I'd rather be writing about horses or my next power tool!) So I can relate to just how much energy it can take to actually develop the skill of being a good conversationalist with each other. But like any other new habit worthy of developing, it can seem awkward, time-consuming, and occasionally, not even worth the effort. I encourage you to keep it up anyway.

I think if you try out this new way of communicating, you'll like the results.

Questions to Consider

1. When you and your spouse talk, do you usually feel heard?

2. Are there differences in communication styles between you?

3. Can you relate to hearing your heart vs. simply hearing your voice?

4. Do you think your spouse usually feels heard by you?

5. Are there changes in your communication you can commit to?

6. On a scale of 1–10 (10, excellent), how are you doing with this habit?

   1___2___3___4___5__-6___7___8___9___10___

7. How do you think your spouse is doing?

   1___2___3___4___5___6___7___8___9___10___

They understand submission.
(Sorry guys…it's not a gender thing.)

Habit #18

They Know When to Be the President and When to Be the Vice President

C ouples in a healthy marriage understand the importance of submission in their relationship. While it may seem similar to the habit suggested in #14, which addressed the importance of considering the needs of the other, the habit of submission is somewhat different since it describes and addresses the process of decision-making that is based on issues such as expertise, experience, and area of strength, rather than on the actual needs of the other.

Certainly, there can be difficult discussions that go into determining who should hold the majority vote in any given decision-making process. And agreeing on this is usually the toughest part of the decision making process. However, once accomplished, coming to an acceptable agreement can be reached more smoothly and with less conflict.

For some—usually men—the thought of an actual "vote" is uncomfortable since it requires discussion, debate, and can lead to disagreement, and for some, a sense of loss of control. So instead of the effort it takes to amicably agree on a path forward, if he doesn't care or have an opinion about the outcome, he simply turns the decision-making over to her.

On the other hand, if he feels strongly about the outcome, he may make the decision unilaterally and expect her to submit to his decision. Neither way encourages discussion that could otherwise lead to a greater sense of teamwork and possibly even a better decision.

So this new habit of "mutual submission" that is usually present in the healthiest of relationships may put a new spin on the idea of submission. In considering this slant on mutual decision-making, it might be helpful to think of shifting positions from president under some circumstances to assuming the role of vice-president when it is called for. And along with that shift of positions, consider the idea of percentage of influence, where the president has a 51 percent vote, and the vice-president has a 49 percent vote. In a healthy relationship, regardless of who the president is in any given decision to be made, both make it a habit of avoiding unilateral decision making and thinking more in terms of mutual submission.

In other words, in a healthy marriage, autocratic decision-making is the exception rather than it is the rule. Rather the emphasis in decision-making is first placed on deciding who should act as president and who will be the vice-president with a minority vote—but a vote nonetheless. This initial decision is often not an easy one and may bring with it some serious discussion and maybe even an argument or two. But once it is clear who and why one should hold a 51 percent say and who will hold the minority vote of 49 percent, well, that's the hard part and usually the rest of the decision making will occur with greater ease.

So in a healthy marriage, how do they achieve the habit of deciding who will have the greater influence (51 percent vs. 49 percent) in the decision-making process?

First, let's get this one out of the way from the start. Sorry guys, but in healthy relationships, who is in charge from situation to situation is not a gender thing (my wife made me clarify this). In marriages where the man plays the gender card—whether it is due to religious conviction, family of origin modeling, or for any other reason—it's not usually a pretty picture these days. "Because I'm your father" doesn't usually work well in parenting; nor does "Because I'm your husband" work in our marriages. At least it doesn't work very well or for very long.

Here are a few examples—simple as they are—of how the president vs. vice-president is determined. In real life, it isn't usually as cut and dried as these examples, but hopefully you will get the idea.

- He does most of the cooking because he enjoys it more and really is the better cook. They go shopping for new pots and pans, and she "just loves" the color of a particular set. He thinks the handles are awkward and unwieldy on the set she likes and not easy to use—who is the president with the 51 percent vote, and who is the vice-president with a 49 percent vote that nonetheless should be heard?

- She does the yard work and wants a particular bush over one he prefers that is much more difficult to maintain— who is the president with the 51 percent vote, and who is the vice-president with a 49 percent that nonetheless should be heard?

- By mutual agreement, he takes the primary role in the finances because she isn't real swift with numbers. When there is a decision to be made over the purchase of one couch that costs twice as much as another, and he says they'd better buy the cheaper one because the more expensive one would cause financial stress—who is the president with the 51 percent vote, and who is the vice-president with a 49 percent vote who nonetheless should be heard?

- She is the primary event coordinator and workhorse when it comes to entertaining. He wants to have friends over for dinner at the end of a week that has been especially difficult and stressful for her. As a result, she is exhausted and would rather have a quiet night to themselves—who is the president with the 51 percent vote, and who is the vice-president with a 49 percent vote that nonetheless should be heard?

- She has recently inherited some money from a long lost but wealthy cousin. In discussing how to use their new-found funds—who is the president with a 51 percent vote, and who is the vice-president with a 49 percent vote that nonetheless should be heard?

Having suggested all of this, it is worth noting that since the president loves the vice-president and is in the habit of considering their needs, there is always room for occasionally overlooking one's larger vote for the wishes of the other. This is in concert with Habit #14 where both consider putting the needs of the other ahead of their own.

While these decisions are a bit simplistic and represent some of the easier ones that couples encounter over the course of their marriage, the process and principles are similar regardless of the complexities many more difficult decisions carry with them.

Questions to Consider

1. Is mutual submission a part of your decision-making process?

2. If not, who usually makes the important decisions in your relationship?

3. Is your current decision-making process acceptable to you?

4. When your spouse is the president, does he/she ever agree to your 49 percent vote anyway?

5. What changes if any would you like to make to your current decision-making process?

6. On a scale of 1–10 (10, excellent), how are you doing with this habit?

   1___2___3___4___5___6___7___8___9___10___

7. How do you think your spouse is doing?

   1___2___3___4___5___6___7___8___9___10___

Control over the other is not a goal.

Habit #19

They Reject the Notion that in Life It Is Either Control or Be Controlled

There are countless issues that motivate couples to seek therapy. Usually those issues they have come in with are actually "symptomatic problems" or secondary symptoms of one or more underlying and usually undetected problems that must eventually be resolved in order to eliminate the current issues that brought them.

One of the more common underlying problems that lead to all sorts of secondary symptoms is the unresolved issue of control, where one person is bent on controlling while the other has finally tired of being controlled. Most are unaware that the real culprit lies beneath the surface and is the problem creating the list of complaints they have come to resolve. So it is understandable that their initial focus and concern are the secondary symptoms that motivated them to seek help in the first place.

Underlying and undetected problems lead to secondary problems (symptoms) that are initially believed to be "the problem." When the underlying issue has to do with control, one or the other may exert it because they believe that's the way it's supposed to be. When he has taken the role of controller, he may justify his control (often labeled "submission" in an effort to make the notion of control more palatable) because "that's what the Bible teaches." Or perhaps it is not so much a religious belief but modeling; "That's what my dad did," or "Well, that's just the way it is supposed to be"—the "me Tarzan, you Jane" mentality.

And control is not always a man thing. Unhealthy and destructive efforts to control can also show up in her efforts as well. One of the most common underlying causes can be that it was the model she grew up with where her mom was the controller in a relationship with a rather weak and subservient father; her sponge-like brain observed and then absorbed: "So *that's* how it's supposed to be!"

So kids who have had issues with control in their childhood years are more likely to grow up having difficulties with it in later adult relationships. While certainly not set in stone and inevitable, they are more likely to adopt one of the two options they have observed and been a part of: they may conclude, "When I grow up, no one is going to control me anymore," or they may believe that being controlled by others must be their lot in life.

These two kids may find their opposites to marry; one who has concluded they are supposed to be under the control of others is often drawn to one who has concluded the solution to being controlled is to be the one in control. After all, these are the roles they have become accustomed to early on.

I must admit that it can be a mystery as to why two young children who have been unduly controlled can come to opposite conclusions—one deciding they will no longer be controlled, the other concluding that being controlled must be their inevitable lot in life. Their opposite conclusions about themselves might, however, be made clearer if we had greater access to the other many variables and experiences that influence the life they end up with. Either way, neither life pattern serves either well.

Whether it is the man or the woman exerting control, when the one being controlled is no longer willing to tolerate the status quo, problematic symptoms like affairs, withdrawal, indifference, overeating, undereating, resentment, and more can rear their ugly head. And these are just a few of the possible secondary difficulties that can motivate their seeking outside help that can take some time and deeper introspection to resolve.

In a healthy marriage, both have gained a good understanding of the destructive role control can play in their relationship. As a result, they make it a habit to avoid the use of control. They have learned too that as a result, many of the secondary symptoms that they came for help with have been resolved.

So be encouraged. The roadmap from our childhood experiences and relationships can still be reshaped and reconfigured.

Questions for Consideration

1. Does control ever play a role in your relationship?

2. How does control (or its absence) affect your marriage?

3. If it is present in your relationship, are you more likely to be the controller or the controlled?

4. What changes regarding control would you like to make?

5. What would those desired changes require of you?

6. On a scale of 1–10 (10, excellent), how are you doing with this habit?

   1___2___3___4___5___6___7___8___9___10___

7. How do you think your spouse is doing?

   1___2___3___4___5___6___7___8___9___10___

Appreciation.

Habit #20

They Recognize the Importance of Appreciating Each Other

When we become accustomed to a positive situation, condition, or perhaps something we have either been given or earned, it is easy for the gratitude and appreciation we might have once had to morph into an attitude of entitlement. It is difficult to appreciate that which we believe we deserve. The thinking may go something like this: "If I am entitled to what I have, then there is no reason to express appreciation." Or maybe we just lost sight of the importance of expressing our gratitude and appreciation.

Most would agree that expressing appreciation for the other is an important and necessary ingredient found in healthy and satisfying relationships. But in spite of what we know is important to the well-being of our marriage, it is easy for the best of us to fall into the habit of feeling entitled rather than expressing appreciation. Or maybe we have just become a bit lazy. Either way, in healthy and satisfying marriages, both are in the habit of regularly showing and speaking their appreciation for the other.

The notion that our relationships could somehow prosper and be mutually satisfying without a significant amount of expressed appreciation seems far-fetched. And yet as the years roll on, and we become accustomed to what we have in the other person, maintaining the habit of expressing our appreciation requires from most of us a greater degree of intentionality. Early on, speaking our appreciation for the other might have been expressed with greater regularity, but over time, it can become easier to take for granted what we have, and our expressing it can fall silent.

Showing appreciation for the unexpected

Showing our appreciation for the "random acts of kindness" that are above and beyond the call of duty is important and may even be easily and consistently expressed. On the other hand, demonstrating our gratitude for those contributions our spouse makes that are necessary and even expected may not come as easily or naturally.

Marriage relationships are full of necessary and expected commitments and obligations that are important for the well-being of the relationship and family. And yet what is expected because it comes with the commitment that was made is less likely to be acknowledged with verbal gratitude since, well, "isn't it expected?" It is easy to adopt the attitude that, if the effort from our spouse is expected and necessary, then expressing our appreciation is somehow unneeded or maybe even undeserved.

Nothing could be further from the truth since expressing appreciation for the efforts of the other—in spite of the fact that those efforts may be expected and even necessary—is vital to the health and well-being of our relationship.

Research in management and business leadership helps support the theory that appreciation for what's expected can play a significant role in motivating people. Studies suggest that even when an underling is required to perform in order to protect their employment, the greater motivation that encourages continued success and excellence is not the fear of termination but rather, the satisfaction that comes when they have been recognized for a job well done, even when their performance was expected.

What Appreciating the Expected Looks Like

"Thanks for being such a great mom." Isn't that what she's supposed to do? Yes, but wouldn't she feel good hearing that you appreciated her doing a great job, even though that's what she's supposed to do?

"Thanks for working so hard and providing us with the life style we have." Isn't that what he's supposed to do? Yes, but wouldn't he/she feel good hearing that you notice and appreciate their efforts, even though that's what you expect?

"I know you are required to help out in Ashley's classroom, but I just want you to know I appreciate your time and effort. You are making a difference." Isn't she required by the school to help out? Yes, but wouldn't she feel good hearing that you value her contribution?

"I know you love coaching Ben and Sam's team, but I still appreciate your being involved that way, even though at the end of your work day, it might feel better to just come home." Doesn't he enjoy coaching so he's doing what he wants to do anyway? Yes, but wouldn't he feel good knowing you appreciate his efforts?

What I often see in marriages that have at one time been stable, growing, and mutually satisfying is the absence of the habit of expressing appreciation for the contributions of the other. Because it is natural to take for granted that which we have grown accustomed to, it becomes more necessary to be intentional in our efforts to express what we appreciate in the other, whether it is for the expected or for the unexpected.

The habit of appreciating has its benefits:

Aside from simply being the right thing to do, there are benefits to be gained in not only making a habit of appreciating the efforts that are above and beyond the call of duty, but those that are expected as well. When we express both more freely, doing so will help us put into greater perspective many of the insignificant complaints we might otherwise dwell on. In other words, expressing our appreciation can help to crowd out the little things that in the long run really don't matter—at least not that much.

When we make it a habit to express our appreciation, we might as well be saying, "I'm thankful I have you." And expressing thankfulness for the other is an all but guaranteed way of building a more successful marriage!

The habit of expressing appreciation helps bolster the confidence of the one we appreciate. It tells them they matter, that they are relevant, and that they make a positive difference in our relationship. Who doesn't want that?

The habit of expressing our appreciation helps guard against the other feeling taken for granted. A common thread that runs throughout many struggling marriages is the complaint that one or both have begun to feel taken for granted and appreciated less since their contributions don't really seem to matter. This then can lead to the secondary or "problematic" symptom of indifference and the loss of motivation needed to continue contributing.

When both are in the habit of expressing their appreciation, their conflicts are usually more easily and quickly resolved because they know that in spite of their momentarily being sideways with each other, they are both still valued.

The list of possible examples of how we could show and express more appreciation is endless, and the benefits are many. Suffice it to say that being recognized and appreciated for a job well done—even if the job is expected and required, and even though we enjoy doing what we're doing—feels good and helps build a happy marriage

Try expressing your appreciation more—not only for what is unexpected and above the call of duty, but for the expected as well. I think you will both like how it feels.

Questions to Consider

1. Is it difficult or is it easy to compliment your spouse? Why?

2. Do you feel adequately appreciated by your spouse?

3. Do you think your spouse feels adequately appreciated by you?

4. How do you think your relationship is affected by the presence/absence of appreciation shown by you both?

5. What are some specific changes you think could be made, if any?

6. On a scale of 1–10 (10, excellent), how are you doing with this habit?

    1___2___3___4___5___6___7___8___9___10___

7. How do you think your spouse is doing?

    1___2___3___4___5___6___7___8___9___10___

There is still passion.

Habit #21

They Work to Keep the Passion in Their Relationship Alive

Consulting my friend Seri, who knows just about everything about everything, she defines passion this way—strong and barely controllable emotions; a sudden outburst of emotions; intense sexual love; an intense desire or enthusiasm for something.

It is worth noting and keeping in mind as you continue reading that only one of the four definitions of passion addresses, well, you know—libido, sexual passion. So when the word *passion* pops up on the following pages, think more broadly about its meaning and how it relates to your relationship. Enthusiasm, involvement, encouragement, support, vulnerability, and yes, libido should be considered when passion is referred to in what follows.

We all love and value the emotions experienced when we are passionate about something. Whether it's our weekly golf game, dabbling in the stock market, our religious faith, a walk on our favorite beach, a deep conversation with a life-long friend, a glass of fine wine, or in my case, an occasional cattle round-up, we experience a great deal of satisfaction when we are passionate about something.

It may be a goal we set out to achieve, along with the excitement and fulfillment that comes when we've accomplished that goal; we may feel passionate about a cause that is of great importance to us; many may be passionate about their life profession, others, about their involvement in volunteer work. Others are passionate and feel a sense of fulfillment that comes along in seeing their parenting efforts producing great and healthy kids.

The list of what generates the passion in our lives seems endless and varies dramatically from one to another; what lights my fire and is a passion of mine might be another's dread. What they might get excited about could very well put me to sleep just thinking about it. Or another's passion may scare me to death! A friend of mine is passionate about hopping on his board and heading straight out to sea for two or three miles before sun up. The phrase "All the tea in China" comes to mind when I wonder what it would take to get me to do such a thing! As long as there's just one shark left in the Pacific, I'm not interested! (By the way and for the record, my seafaring friend may be scared silly of horses, a passion that comes naturally to me.)

So one man's passion is another man's indifference. However, there is one life event that we have in common and can all relate to and that is the passionate experience of discovering a new and hope-fully romantic relationship. Can't we all relate to that memory? It went something like this:

At the beginning of our newly discovered relationship, it was just about the only thing we could think about or focus on. The pas-sion we initially felt consumed us; we became forgetful; we stopped going out with the boys (or the girls) in order to be with this new relationship. Other things that once were of importance to us seemed no longer to matter that much; our new flame walked in, and we immediately focused on her—and there might just as well have been no one else in the room; she spoke, we listened; she needed some-thing, we jumped.

She had a hard time sleeping at night because she was thinking about how great the day with him had been; she looked forward to the next time they would be together, often at the expense of what she was currently involved in.

You remember the feeling—and it certainly was not initially a feeling of commitment to your new relationship that drew the two of you together! *You were turned on and you know it!* It may not have completely been a function of libido, but the motivation of commitment had nothing to do with your relationship when you first met. Commitment early in your relationship was unnecessary since passion based on first impressions and early experiences was all that was required to keep the relationship afloat and on fire.

You liked the way she breathed. She could do no wrong. Yes, she took you by storm, and you were putty in her hands because of the passion you felt for her. It might or might not have happened over night, but it did happen. Otherwise, your relationship would not have continued. It would have ended like all the others.

Let's face it. During those early days of courtship, passion, and all that was involved in the "mating dance" was all that was needed to keep the relationship afloat. And we were very close to useless when it came to any other endeavors. She was a babe, he was a stud (well, at least a reasonable facsimile!), and you both loved the way the other looked, talked, walked, and ate. You were even drawn to each other's quirks.

So it was because of the passion we felt that our relationship seemed to evolve with such great ease. And not only was there nothing wrong with the early and initial passion that attracted us, there was in fact, something very right and good about it; after all, without it, there would likely have been little to draw us to each other. It is doubtful that after our first glance, any of us said to ourselves, "Now *there's* someone I could really commit to!" No, it was passion, but it is probably a good thing that its original intensity did not last forever. Otherwise, we'd accomplish very little else in our lives today.

(Sometimes I surprise myself. After writing the last couple of pages, I think I'll try my hand at a romance novel!)

Our ability to be passionate is one of life's experiences that sets us apart from other creatures in the animal world; experiencing passion is a part of what makes us who we are, and it is meant to be a part of our life experience. So it stands to reason that passion in our marriage is not meant to be a temporary jumpstart but instead, an ongoing part that nurtures our marriage relationship. While not at the same intensity (remember, would any of us accomplish much of anything if we lived in that initial bliss forever?), keeping the passion alive is not only possible but it is essential to the health and well-being of our relationship.

So then why does it seem to dissipate—or in too many marriages, disappear altogether these days? Is passion really intended only as initial fuel for a new relationship and then like retro rockets on a trip to the moon, meant to be eliminated?

Contrary to the old adage, "All good things must come to an end," a realistic and significant degree of passion in our marriage need not come to an end just because real life shows up. Unfortunately for so many though, that's precisely what happens—real life shows up. And it is unfortunate that for far too many, their marriage ends because the passion ends, leaving them both asking, "What happened to the love we once shared?"

In general terms, this is what happened: first, it is easy to confuse and equate those early stages of passion with "being in love." So when the intensity of the passion in a relationship is inevitably affected and begins to decrease due to life happening, this loss of passion can be misunderstood as "I must be falling out of love. It just isn't the same as it used to be." This disillusionment can lead to all sorts of poor choices and dysfunctional behaviors, and the marriage can fall victim to the proverbial self-fulfilling prophecy.

The second thing that can happen is this: early on, maintaining a high and fulfilling level of passion took little effort (it was like picking the low-lying fruit on a tree. It was all so easy, so effortless), so it is easy to assume falsely that maintaining that original level of passion should continue to be somewhat effortless and ever-present; when they realize it takes much more intentional energy, they may fall prey to the false assumption that "I must be falling out of love," "I must have married the wrong person." The consequences of such false assumptions can lead to all sorts of poor choices and dysfunctional behaviors that in turn lead to very painful and destructive self-fulfilling consequences.

The Influence and Necessity of Commitment When Life Kicks In

So what do couples in a healthy and fulfilling marriage fall back on when the realities of life show up and threaten their original passion? What keeps their relationship not only afloat but thriving?

When the bills mount up, when she doesn't turn off the lights behind her, when he fails to put the toilet seat down because it just isn't that important to him, when she expects more reassurance than he thinks she should need, when the baby and sleepless nights arrive, when she tells him how to drive, when kids take up the time they once spent with each other, when she observes his second glance at an attractive waitress—how do they keep their relationship alive?

As our original passion is inevitably impacted by the realities of life, the influence of commitment must come into play and provide the foundation that supports and nurtures the relationship. And what is required to sustain a significant level of passion is not just a commitment to the institution of marriage but to the person we are in the marriage relationship with as well. Only then are we able to put in the effort it takes to keep the passion alive; commitment to the institution of marriage is simply not enough.

When commitment to each other is weak or not in the mix at all, maintaining a healthy and realistic degree of passion during the challenging times of life becomes even more difficult. So it is commitment during the good and easy times as well as the bad and difficult ones that provides the foundation for keeping the passion alive. And yes, passion in spite of many years of marriage *is* possible, but usually not without a good deal of work and effort at times that in the beginning might have been unnecessary.

So what are the specific efforts needed in order to keep the passion alive in our marriage? At the risk of repeating myself (which I am about to do), many of the necessary efforts could be wrapped up by reviewing the previous twenty habits you've just read about. While there is certainly more that can and should be done in order to keep the passion alive and well, reviewing what has been suggested here is a good place to start.

Keeping the passion alive takes giving some thought to what really matters before we complain.

It takes working hard to avoid grudges by productively addressing issues and complaints that really do matter.

It takes humbling ourselves when we have blown it and asking to be forgiven for our imperfection.

It takes humbling ourselves enough to take the risk of offering forgiveness when forgiveness is asked for (and maybe even when it isn't asked for).

It takes looking more diligently for the things in life to laugh about—and then laughing about them. As importantly, it takes being willing to laugh at ourselves from time to time.

It takes not only appreciating but also celebrating our personality differences.

It takes vulnerability.

It takes truly enjoying and being thankful for our spouse's good fortune and moments of recognition.

It takes abandoning the attitude of "good guy-bad guy" during times of conflict.

It takes the mutual goal and desire to solve the problem rather than the desire to win the argument.

It takes acting/reacting, behaving, talking, and in general, living as if today were your last together.

It takes knowing and acknowledging we have baggage and then working to minimize the influence it has on our relationship.

It takes consistently considering the needs of our spouse as every bit as important as ours.

It takes going public once in a while (otherwise known as bragging) with what it is about our spouse we are proud of.

It takes having fun together, even if it might take more intentional effort to make the fun times happen.

It takes communicating in such a way that we not only hear the words of the other but their heart as well.

It takes knowing what it means to be mutually submissive and then practicing it.

It takes rejecting the notion of "control or be controlled."

And finally, it takes understanding the importance of appreciating not only the unexpected efforts that are above and beyond the call of duty but appreciating what is expected from our spouse as well.

Questions to Consider

1. What current "life experiences" interfere most with the passion that you once had in your relationship?

2. Are you satisfied with the degree of passion in your relationship?

3. For you, what would it take to increase the passion in your marriage?

4. What would it take from you to improve the passion in your marriage?

5. Is commitment alive and well even when there are dips in the passion?

6. On a scale of 1–10 (10, excellent), how are you doing with this habit?

   1__2__3__4__5__6__7__8__9__10__

7. How do you think your spouse is doing?

   1__2__3__4__5__6__7__8__9__10__

Conclusion

So there you have it. Just about everything you ever wanted or needed to know about what it takes to achieve a new and improved marriage relationship. Well, maybe not *all* you need to know, but certainly all *I* know! But hopefully now you know much more of what goes into a satisfying and more fulfilling marriage—one you always wanted-and maybe once had.

There has seldom been a book written for the purpose of helping the reader improve their lot in life that made much difference or was helpful, unless the effort of reading was followed by hard and disciplined work. Without application, knowledge is useless. The real success and satisfaction come out of actually implementing a new and intentional plan of action.

So I encourage you to do just that. Having taken the time and making the effort to read about the importance of replacing old habits that work against your relationship with new ones that will improve it, now work together to implement some new behaviors that you both decide will lead to a better and more satisfying marriage.

Be creative. Don't limit the possibilities of new habits in your relationship to what has been suggested here. Talk together about any new efforts you believe could lead to an improvement in your relationship.

Review together from time to time the twenty-one habits found in healthy and successful marriages. Occasionally revisit and discuss the questions provided at the end of each of the twenty-one habits as well. This will help you evaluate progress you have made as a result of your efforts. And doing so will also serve as a reminder that the goal in all of this is to maintain a process rather than to reach a destination.

Any feedback, stories to share, suggestions, or criticisms will be greatly appreciated.

Ed Wimberly, Ph.D.
Docedwimberly@gmail.com

About the Author

E d Wimberly, PhD, began his professional career in private practice forty-five years ago in Santa Barbara, California. After earning a bachelor's degree from Westmont College, he went on to receive a master's degree in clinical psychology from Arizona State University (ASU) and then a Ph.D. from United States International University (USIU) in San Diego, California.

His practice consists of treating not only individuals but couples who are struggling in their marriages as well, and it is his observations made in his work that provides the backdrop for what his book addresses.

Ed is the proud father of two grown and wonderful daughters, Ashley and Allyson, and a grandfather to two equally wonderful grandsons, Ben and Sam. He has been married to Joan, the love of his life, for forty-eight years.

Ed is also the author of *Parenting with an Attitude...21 Questions Successful Parents Ask Themselves* and continues in his private practice with individuals and couples in Santa Barbara. To maintain his own sanity, he likes to run (okay, trot), ride horses, play golf, constantly redo his home landscaping, and spend time with Joan.

CPSIA information can be obtained
at www.ICGtesting.com
Printed in the USA
FSHW021456121119
64014FS